PRAISE FOR
MASTERING YOUR INNER CRITIC

The school of hard knocks is a great testing ground for the most insightful research, and Susan's book proves that putting the two together facilitates personal action planning for the many women trying to advance in today's challenging workplace. I recommend this book to women who have committed their careers to organizational life.

—Helen Drinan, President,
Simmons College

Susan Brady serves up the secret sauce for the 21st century purposeful leader. This timely and inspiring book advances the purpose movement from talk to walk.

—Richard Leider, internationally bestselling
author of *The Power of Purpose, Repacking
Your Bags* and *Life Reimagined*

Susan is an exceptional leader in her own right, and her willingness to be transparent about her own hurdles is honest, engaging, and highly effective at encouraging the same in all leaders—myself included.

—Alan Webber, Mayor, Santa Fe, New Mexico
and cofounder of Fast Company Magazine

Too many women live with a relentless Inner Critic who wakes them up at night, tells them they aren't good enough, and haven't proven they deserve more. Read this, embrace your strengths, and release the inner joy that will define your success.

—Suzanne Bates, author of *All the Leader
You Can Be* and *Speak Like a CEO*

Susan Brady has drawn from her own experience as a successful female leader, as well as years of experience working with others, to craft an important contribution to the field of leadership. In *Mastering Your Inner Critic* she demonstrates how women leaders have the power to create their own path to advancement through understanding both themselves and the reality of the world they're dealing with. Susan's book is not only a must-read for any woman who wants to expand their capacity to grow as a leader, but is valuable for men as well!

—Howard J. Ross, author of *Everyday Bias*
and *Our Search for Belonging*

With spectacular clarity and an empathic heart for women, Susan Brady calls attention to and delivers actionable solutions for an insidious ingredient in the psyche of even the most externally confident women: the Inner Critic. For those women smart and self-aware enough to pick up this book, a path to mental peace and confidence has finally been forged.

—Juliet Funt,
CEO of WhiteSpace at Work

The bad news: our internal critic reinforces seven hurdles that specifically obstruct women's advancement. The good news: we can deactivate our critic by reconnecting with our Compassionate Center. Clear and practical, Susan's book combines diagnostic work with self-help training. Susan extracts lessons from books, one-on-one conversations with experts, and her own experience to offer a three-step method to empower women: identify your thoughts and emotions, press the pause button, then access your Compassionate Center, which always knows you are complete and perfect beyond your human limitations.

—Jamil Mahuad,
Former President of the Republic of Ecuador

Susan speaks with a clarity and passion that resonates with leaders everywhere. Combining insights from her personal leadership journey and her extensive research, Susan's practical book raises the bar of possibility for women and men who aspire to create ever-increasing impact—in the workplace, and in the world.

—Saj-nicole Joni, internationally acclaimed CEO, advisor, and strategist, and author of the bestselling *Get Big Things Done: The Power of Connectional Intelligence*

Susan Brady has trained thousands of executives in conflict resolution and relationship management and has facilitated solutions to hundreds of complex business situations. Her book is filled with practical wisdom and motivating stories from real women and will enable you to believe that you have the power to change your own path to advancement. A must-read for any woman who knows she's capable of so much more.

—Larraine Segil, Chairman and CEO of Exceptional Women Awardees Foundation

Brady's book is the perfect blend of an overarching strategy to help you think about achieving your next level and the tactics to break down barriers that so often block people from realizing their full potential.

—Jeremy Gutsche, *New York Times* bestselling author of *Better and Faster*

Susan Brady's remarkable book provides many powerful insights for women leaders. With directness and wisdom, she addresses one of the most common pitfalls facing women in their professional lives: their Inner Critic. Susan offers key tools that will create breakthroughs and personal, lasting fulfillment. A must-read for all women.

—Barbara Annis, Founder and CEO, The Gender Intelligence Group

Susan Brady has given voice to the critical barriers that impede women leaders from the full realization of their talents and gifts. In an unapologetic, transparent conversation, Susan calls out the barriers and provides easy to execute remedies that will propel readers to their leadership reality!

—Carla A. Harris, Vice Chairman, Managing Director and Senior Client Advisor at Morgan Stanley

I can't think of a woman who won't benefit from reading Susan Brady's new book. The Inner Critic is a toxic force that can hold even the most accomplished woman back. But Susan shows not only how to silence that destructive voice, but how to deal with its impact on our ability to create work that is sustainable, energizing, and rewarding. We all need to celebrate this—and to read it!

—Sally Helgesen, coauthor with Marshall Goldsmith of the bestselling *How Women Rise* and coauthor of *The Female Advantage*

I have seen Susan's work on the Inner Critic and the 7 Hurdles touch the lives of women at Toyota in deeply meaningful ways. This book is a must-read for all leaders and especially for women who aspire to greater levels of leadership impact.

—Mike Groff, Former President and CEO Toyota Financial Services and Lexus Financial Services

What we love about this book is how *practical* it is. It's not a vague theory for how to clear life's hurdles. Brady is on the track with us, coaching us each step of the way.

—Sheila Heen and Douglas Stone, coauthors of the *New York Times* bestseller *Difficult Conversations*

I wish the leadership lessons in this book could somehow be put in our water supply. People—and especially women—would get more out of their lives by returning to this book over and over again.

—Brigadier General Tom Kolditz, PhD, Professor Emeritus, U.S. Military Academy, West Point, founding Executive Director, Doerr Institute for New Leaders

MASTERING
YOUR INNER
CRITIC
AND 7 OTHER
HIGH HURDLES TO ADVANCEMENT

HOW THE BEST WOMEN LEADERS
PRACTICE SELF-AWARENESS TO
CHANGE WHAT REALLY MATTERS

SUSAN MACKENTY BRADY

NEW YORK   CHICAGO   SAN FRANCISCO
ATHENS   LONDON   MADRID
MEXICO CITY   MILAN   NEW DELHI
SINGAPORE   SYDNEY   TORONTO

1 2 3 4 5 6 7 8 9   QVS   23 22 21 20 19 18

ISBN 978-1-260-44060-7
MHID   1-260-44060-5

e-ISBN 978-1-260-44061-4
e-MHID   1-260-44061-3

Library of Congress CIP
Names: Brady, Susan (Susan McKenty), author.
Title: Mastering your inner critic... and 7 other high hurdles to advancement : how the best women leaders practice self-awareness to change what really matters / by Susan Brady.
Description: New York : McGraw-Hill, [2019] | Includes bibliographical references.
Identifiers: LCCN 2018039327| ISBN 9781260440607 (alk. paper) | ISBN 1260440605
Subjects: LCSH: Women executives. | Self-perception. | Leadership. | Career development. | Women—Vocational guidance. | Success.
Classification: LCC HD6054.3 .B73 2019 | DDC 658.4/092082—dc23 LC record available at https://lccn.loc.gov/2018039327.

McGraw-Hill Education books are available at special quantity discounts to use as premiums and sales promotions or for use in corporate training programs. To contact a representative, please visit the Contact Us pages at www.mhprofessional.com.

For Caroline & Abigail:
May your Inner Critic coach be masterful,
and may you scale any hurdles you face in life
with confidence & grace.

CONTENTS

FOREWORD

All too well, I know what it feels like to reach for perfection and define your worth by action and achievement alone. I was a straight A student and never got a B from the 6th grade through graduate school. This academic track record is rooted in my thinking that being loved and being worthy were predicated on achieving and producing. All of my self-worth was rooted in what I did and less about who I was. I carried this frame of mind into my professional life, where it became a huge hurdle.

With an inability to empower people and watch them grow, I finally realized that placing such value on what I singularly did was really the opposite of leadership. It came from a good place, but I was not making the people around me better as long as I was insisting on doing it all by myself. When I think of my own journey, and now I have the absolute privilege of being a VP in a really big company, none of this would have been possible without figuring out that I didn't have to *do it all*. Unknowingly, I had been functioning in a selfish way. It was a hard reality check for me when I realized I was hurting people around me and limiting their ability to grow. That I was over-rowing and feeling overwhelmed, which effectively impeded my ability to lead.

As soon as I got that, everything shifted. When I started to derive my joy and satisfaction from watching others step into new things and do certain things that historically I had done, that was a huge shift. Everything changed.

Now that I have the language for it, thanks to Susan, the best way I can describe the Inner Critic and what I want to say to women I work with, mentor, coach, or partner with is: "If you could only see yourself the way I see you!" I see their own Inner Critics playing out every day, holding them back from their capacity and contributions.

The biggest hurdle these women face is holding themselves back as a result of the other hurdles described in Susan's book: proving your value, clarity, recognized confidence, and more. Yes, there are systems that make advancement more difficult sometimes, but consider the following example as a snapshot of what we're up against when it comes to the Inner Critic leaving a trail of damage and destruction if left unchecked:

When a company like Toyota ventures down the road of doing formal sponsorship, such as our women's advancement program, Success Share, it's an immense undertaking. Before this program manifested, the most pressing consideration (and I've heard this from other companies, too) was, *if we ordain these women as being worthy of sponsorship and advancing their careers, then they are going to feel entitled. What if we can't deliver on this promise?* With Susan as my witness, this could not have been further from the truth.

We launched the program, notified the selected women, superior performers who should have already been operating a level above where they were, and brought them into the room on the first day. Susan opened the event with, "How did you feel when Kim called you to inform you that you were going to be part of this inaugural program, Success Share?" The outcome was unbelievable to me, and I will never forget this. She went person to person and two reactions were consistent: There were tears. Partially of gratitude and partially from feeling unworthy. Again, these are the best of the best, and their initial response was, "Wait! It's me?" Then the next question out of their mouths was, "How much more can I do to make sure that I prove I was the right choice? How much harder can I work?"

As a leader of HR, the reason this example is so important is the scale of that untapped contribution from 20 high-achieving women who didn't feel worthy. How many people aren't stepping into the right position because they aren't sure of their skills or impact?

This concept of recognizing how much you are capable of and giving all you have to give is quite significant. As I looked at all these women, again I thought, *If you saw yourself the way I do!* At the end of that year, because we focused on the hurdles and Linkage's outstanding model, we talked about recognized confidence, having clarity, and making the ask. With this level of self-awareness and a new language assigned to their own challenges, I saw these women blossom.

HR is my passion. Every job I've done, 11 or 12 roles over the years, I loved. This is my purpose so, when I got promoted to VP recently, I was full of clarity and confidence. Not long after my appointment, I learned that we would be moving our headquarters from California to Texas. Everything about this move would impact people. Their lives would be turned upside down.

Would they move to a new state and stay with Toyota? For most people, there is no easy answer. Then my Inner Critic seized the moment. "How will you make sure you do this right? You're not prepared for this—you've never led a company through this specific challenge! And you will be leading a team to support the organization and they will have the same life-altering decisions. You're not the right person!"

For twenty-four hours, I did this painful wrangling with myself.

Then my rational side took over, reminding me of Susan's talk at Linkage's Women in Leadership Institute™. I pushed PAUSE. My Compassionate Center took hold. I realized:

"Kim, no, you have never done this before, but you care so deeply about the people who work here and the values we live and breathe at Toyota. Who you are and what you bring will see you through." There was this shift. I could do this! It was the training, language, education, and self-awareness—not only in what I would feel challenged by, but also being able to claim what I'm good at—that allowed me to step up and tackle this hurdle. I will never again have a career experience that has stakes that high or such huge implications for a company and for literally thousands of people. That is just a recent example of what mastering these hurdles meant for me.

Susan has taught me how to pause when my Inner Critic takes over. Now, I literally think of that red PAUSE button in my head and push it! It helps me stop. By listening more rather than thinking I'm right, I can get the most out of what others have to offer. And by articulating my thoughts rather than stewing in feeling not good enough, I ensure that I'm not withholding something of value I can contribute. It sounds simple, but it has been extremely meaningful.

Susan's impact, her insight, her honesty and willingness to speak the truth, without exception, is very easily taken in, in a loving way. I have seen people's lives change. Watching Susan's impact, insight, and coaching, not just with others but with me, has made people's lives better. When you're better at work and contributing in a way that makes a difference, when you're being stretched, when you're accomplishing things that are meaningful, when someone believes in you, you're a better parent and partner. This is work that changes people's lives. Not just by making them effective at work, but more effective in all facets of our lives. When you unburden yourself of all that self-talk and criticism, you'll be better everywhere.

This stuff matters. It genuinely changes people's lives. That is what gets me out of bed every morning. I care about our business. We are a for-profit company. We do amazing things for the world, no question. At the end of the day though, touching people's lives every day and knowing people are better in some way, that is this work. Then there are the business benefits. People are bringing everything they have to offer. You move the company forward in ways you can't put a price tag on.

Susan's very specific role is that she has an unbelievable gift: being able to put words to things that people have a hard time articulating, and attaching language to them that enables us to work through things in a different way or put a label on them so you can let go and move past them. Her ability to sift through the clutter and get to the heart of the matter is like no one I have ever encountered. This book encompasses all that Susan offers, and it *will* make you better.

Kim Cerda
Vice President, Human Resources
and Operational Excellence
Toyota Financial Services

ACKNOWLEDGMENTS

"Did I get everyone? Oh my—how I don't want to forget anyone. So many brilliant and generous souls have a right to see this as their work too. How (on earth) can I honor the time and effort others made to help this book come to life? How will I appreciate the sacrifice my husband and daughters have made while I have been semi-obsessed with this topic (how best to help women get out of their own way— myself included) for the last five years? How can I express gratitude to my family, friends, mentors, teachers, and the lifetime of colleagues from whom I have learned and grown?"

Pause. Breathe, Susan. You got this . . .

THE AWESOME LITERARY MIDWIVES

The work that is involved in writing a book is daunting. I compare it to pregnancy. We simply don't know what we're getting into until we are with child. I was lucky to have not one but *three* midwives to help bring this project to life. (Note, to those reading who have not been in the care of a midwife: this is the person who creates calm in the worst of the storm, who has vast experience advising on *exactly what you are trying to do*, who coaches you along the way, whose judgement and leadership you must follow if you wish to live through it to see the other side, all so that there is a successful outcome.)

The first of my literary midwives is the very gifted editor Donya Dickerson of McGraw-Hill. It was Donya to whom I sent the very first proposal for this book. Not only did she not reject it, she took time to explain what it would take for the project to be published—including partnering with an expert writer. She told me to come back to her once I did as she suggested. I did. Donya championed this work at McGraw-Hill and I am honored to be published by such an esteemed and deeply-rooted publishing house, but even more so to call you, Donya, my editor.

The second midwife is Candi Sue Cross. Candi: without your talent and amazing eye for the written word, this book simply would not be. It was you that heard, affirmed, and enjoyed *all* of what I had to say on any given subject, person, or hurdle and painstakingly refined my often verbose expression into something more succinct (and grammatically correct). You went the extra mile, you worked with me in the wee hours.

The third midwife is Kari Black, who coordinated all editorial goodness as part of the McGraw-Hill team. Kari edited every page and managed the production process, ensuring that our raw manuscript turned into the book you're holding now.

To all three of you: Thank you so much for believing this book would make a difference, and for being my partners in bringing it to life.

THE AWESOME FAMILY

The energy and heart that went into this book would not have been possible without the support, wisdom, and love from my family—not just in the birthing of the book, but over my lifetime.

Thank you, Jamie Brady, my generous, humble, and wise husband, for challenging me to play big, and for loving me fully even while I leave our oasis to dance in the world to awaken some spirit. Thank you, Caroline & Abbie, for being glorious you, understanding your place in my life (first), and for also appreciating at a young age the meaning and purpose with which each day can be lived. It is these three who found me at the kitchen table in most "spare" moments typing away—waking in the morning to an over-caffeinated wife and mother asking simply, "Did you wake up at 4:00 a.m. again?" Thank you, Sarah Kroll, our partner in crime for all things "Casa Brady." Over the past year, you kept our home life sane, children fed, dog walked, and did so with grace and calm.

Thank you, Mardee Moore, my very encouraging and loving mother, whose vibrant, positive, and caring nature inspires me to see a world full of blessings. Thank you, my curious and ferociously upbeat step-father, David Moore, for showing me so much of the way; your belief in my potential has made its mark in my life. To my hilarious and loving brother, Bill MacKenty: Thank you for accepting me fully and laughing with me at all that is bananas about life. Thank you Dagmara MacKenty, my beautiful and wise sister, for being a healing voice of reason—always. Thank you, Maria MacKenty, for supporting me and believing in me—even in those not-so-easy teenage years. Connie Brady—thank you for being the very essence of a strong female role model, a voice of support for me and my work, and an all-around great mother-in-law. Thank you, Jennifer Meade. You ground me, laugh with me, play with me, drink wine with me, and tell me the truth like none other! Last but not least: Thank you Jerry MacKenty—for dedicating the better part of your life to raising up kids who felt loved, and for telling me to go for it. You are my angel, my guide. I miss you every day.

THE AWESOME CONTRIBUTORS

This book would not have been made manifest without the extraordinary people who work for and receive the goodness of Linkage. Sourced mainly through Linkage's Women in Leadership Institute, I thank the thousands of women leaders who have experienced the impact of coming together and learning to lead themselves, and the hundreds of brilliant thought leaders and speakers over the years. You are the foundation of the field research that led to the 7 Hurdles. The women I feature in this book range from clients to experts who I have had the privilege of working for or with, all who have been a source of inspiration to me and others. All of these women are leaders worth following, and it is my honor to bring their voices to life on the page and share their gifts with you. Thank you, Abri Holden, Tara Swart, Cynthia Tragge-Lakra, Melissa Master-Holder, Michelle Webb, Sarah Bettman, Yolanda Conyers, Shannon Arnold, Joanne Brem, Darlene Slaughter, Yasmin Davidds, Stephanie Roemer, Kristy Roberts, Amy Bladen Shatto, Barbara Annis, Sabreen Dhillon, Sonya Jacobs, Margie Warrell, and Madelyn Yucht.

And there are men too, who have helped me hone my own thinking and their own contribution shows up in the pages of this book either explicitly or implicitly. These are the men with whom I have had many conversations in recent years about women in leadership, my own path or theirs in leadership, or leadership generally and the role men play in the advancement of women. Thank you, Charley Morrow, Mark Hannum, Stu Cohen, Greg Zlevor, Mitchell Nash, Sam Lam, Devon Brown, Dave Vaughn, Bernardus Holtrop, Andy Bird, Bill Frew, Mike Groff, Mike Wells, Pete Carey, Seth Smiley, Dave Logan, Richard Leider, Glenn Llopis, Howard Ross, Sean Kavanagh, Buzz Waterhouse, Jeff Brinkman, Scott Sherman, Mark Rutherford, Jamil Mahuad, Jon Magnuson, Bill Springer, Harold Weinstein, Rick Pumfrey, Reed Parker, Chris Cappy, Thomas Crahan, and Dr. Rudy Ansbacher.

THE AWESOME
WISE AUTHOR "ELDERS"

Taking a page from neuroscientist Dr. Tara Swart's wisdom (Chapter 4, on the hurdle of Clarity)—when confronted with doing something big that we have never done before (like writing a book) our brain needs to believe *we can do it*. For this, says Dr. Swart, we need to "borrow" our confidence from others who have succeeded in doing the "big thing" we haven't yet. If they can do it, so can I? Alas, every step of the way, the universe provided what turned out to be my own "book advisory board" of incredibly successful published authors—each one of them I admire deeply; each one of them gave me invaluable wisdom along the way. To you, Dave Logan, Carla Harris, Saj-nicole Joni, Alan Webber, Margie Warrell, Tom Kolditz, and Richard Leider— my heartfelt gratitude for your time and coaching.

THE AWESOME COLLEAGUES

So many talented colleagues at Linkage have played a role in honing the wisdom found in this book. Without Ellen Wingard, Linkage's work in the space of Women's Leadership would likely not be. Phil Harkins envisioned Linkage's one-day impact in the field of Women's Leadership. Harley Ostis approved and encouraged the development of a consulting practice on Advancing Women Leaders. Matt Norquist dreamed up the metaphor of the hurdles, and ultimately made this book possible—supporting me every step of the way. Thank you, Jennifer McCollum, for seeing and supporting this project over the finish line. Jill Ihsanullah brilliantly created the assessments and metrics around which Linkage's field research was validated and took the work to another stratosphere altogether. Briana Goldman and Shirley Milgram researched and built so much of the modular content that marries to the hurdles. Shannon Bayer and Abri Holden spent endless hours with me codifying the work on Coaching Your Inner Critic. Stu Cohen was the first brave man who raised his hand to become an expert facilitator in Coaching the Inner Critic and applied his own twist. Sarah Dayton-McGlinchey engaged many of Linkage's clients, powerfully building credibility and becoming every bit an expert on the advancement of women. Thank you, Sarah, for diving in the deep end with me on all of this work. Kristin Barrett championed with grace the commitment of many new clients in this work. Rachael Marangu took the Women in Leadership Client Advisory Board—and our business—to another level altogether. Kerry Seitz: your steady hand as our Women in Leadership Institute (WIL)™ leader is and will continue to bring this work to even more women the world over. Sarah Breigle, you were there when the thought of Coaching the Inner Critic was birthed; a willing and supportive partner every step of the way.

Susie Kelleher, Scott Gavriel, Desley Khew, Paula Butte, Lizzette Lima, Rita Buscher, Maria Auperin, Muriel Jones, Karina Wilhelms, Danielle Lucido, and Dana Yonchak—your support and wisdom has played an important role in Linkage's unique place in the Advancing Women Leaders arena. Thank you, Amy Kimball, for all you do to help so much work better at Linkage—and for all you have done for my world especially.

I thank those friends and colleagues, in addition to those listed above, who I have been lucky enough to work with and learn from outside of Linkage. Kim Cerda, your courage and executive advocacy to foster real change for women has been awe inspiring and it is an honor to call you a friend and partner. Thank you Jagdish Parihk, Stu Kliman, Michele Gravelle, Amy Fox, Erica Ariel Fox, Tod Beaty, Julie Salganik, Susan Vroman, Terry Real, Lisa Merlo Booth, Jan Bergstrom, Jack Kaklowski, Lisa Sullivan, Wendy Whelihan, Cher Stout, Ashley Wollam, Adam Rothberg, Laura Stone, Nick Craig, Elaine Stokes, Shannon O'Mara, Kathleen Bochman, Kelly Smith, Nancy Ban, Kendra Angier, Emily Lundi-Mallett, Richlynn Baily, Katherine Adkins, Julia Wada, Karen Ideno, Karen Wetherholt, Toni Handler, Jodi Ecker Detjen, Michelle Waters, Sandy Asch, Linnea Burman, Nancie Torrance, Margaret Keene, Mary Ellen

Kassotakis, Karla Wiseman, Jan Shubert, Elaine Ward, Margaret Gyetko, Aida Sabo, April Mason, Kelly Gerlach, Heather Updegraff, Kelly Brown, and Ray Keane.

All of these people have helped me and this work mature to what it is. Each of you has influenced my thinking; your wisdom is in the pages of this book, in my daily practices, and thus in my head and heart. My wish is that this book pays all that forward.

THE AWESOME SISTERHOOD

I don't have a large group of friends with whom I gather on weekends. My tribe of sisters are geographically dispersed and *kick-ass*, each and every one. While I have lived the field research of this book and the realities of working and mothering for years, I don't get to see or connect with you as often as I want. You remain the women with whom I have laughed and cried the most. Thank you for loving me over the years and giving me the gift and wisdom of your friendship. You know who you are, and my life is richer because you are in it.

———

Did I get everyone? I'm pretty sure I did. And for those who I didn't mention but with whom I have connected over the years, know that your impact is in these pages somewhere too. (She says, from Compassionate Center . . .)

CHAPTER 1

LEARNING
TO GLIDE

WAIT. YOU WANT ME TO HURDLE?

Every story has a beginning. When I set out to clarify what was going on for women with whom I was working, I focused at first on the many ways to awaken them to their full leadership potential. Over time, however, what emerged were things that represent unique challenges for women on their leadership journeys. But what I didn't know was what I should call those unique challenges. How could I label those "things" in a way that would capture their uniqueness for women? How could I give them a name that could also be powerfully congruent with the intentional actions needed to get over, around, through, or beyond these things? Should they be Barriers? Obstacles? Pitfalls? Challenges? Yucky Stuff?

I am not a runner, and I am sure not a hurdler. I actually thought hurdles were jumped over by the runner. I was wrong. Thanks to a chance conversation with a former colleague who was a nationally competitive track and fielder, I had one of those wonderful aha moments: I found out that you don't jump over hurdles. If you're a hurdler, you learn to run with long, powerful strides. With a lot of practice and stumbling and crashing, you learn to be ready for a hurdle and to glide over it, spending as little time as possible in the air. You master getting your feet back under you quickly and confidently—and you keep on running with confidence—until the next hurdle.

"That's it!" I thought. That's what it feels like for women on their journey to leadership advancement. For me, this captured so much of what I have experienced myself, what I've learned from other women over the years, and what I've learned from the wealth of research out there.

We all face unique hurdles that are sometimes unexpected, hidden, or incredibly high. And as women in the workplace we face each new hurdle while simultaneously running full tilt to clear the hurdles we've already mastered: Performing our assigned roles, taking on complex new assignments and projects, making strategic decisions, working with others, etc., etc., etc. While we may be lucky enough to get some training along the way that can help us identify and maybe even anticipate certain hurdles, we don't often get the real-deal kind of insights or coaching we need for what it will take to run and glide over them.

But what if, no one clued you in to the presence of hurdles to begin with? What if, even when you realize there are hurdles, you feel alone and confused, or even ashamed because you don't know what to do? What if you tried various approaches but kept failing? What if there was this nagging, whining voice in your head that kept whispering, "This is dumb. It doesn't matter," or even worse, "I'm dumb. I don't matter."

So with the metaphor of "hurdles" in hand, I got to work—ultimately creating this book. It's my way of sharing what my colleagues at Linkage and I have learned about eight unique and often hidden hurdles women face. Insight about each of these eight hurdles comes from a distillation of the findings from Linkage's evaluative data of the more than 10,000 women and 2,500 multi-raters who have attended Linkage's Women in Leadership Institute over the last 18 years, plus interviews with talent and diversity leaders from Fortune 500 companies.

WE WOMEN HAVE WORK TO DO

Most women I know who aspire to positions of leadership have drive, intelligence, and the will to work their tails off. Here's the problem: We, as women, aren't advancing nearly at the rate we want to or our organizations need us to.

The World Economic Forum's 2017 Global Gender Gap Report benchmarked 144 countries on their progress towards gender parity across four thematic dimensions: Economic Participation and Opportunity, Educational Attainment, Health and Survival, and Political Empowerment. "Weighted by population, in 2017, the average progress on closing the global gender gap stands at 68.0%—meaning an average gap of 32.0% remains to be closed worldwide across the four Index dimensions in order to achieve universal gender parity, compared to an average gap of 31.7% last year."

My colleagues and I at Linkage have come to learn a great deal about which organizational efforts can accelerate the advancement of women in leadership. We're proud and excited to see many of our client organizations experience progress in their efforts to create gender parity in leadership as a result of our working together.

Dr. Jillian Maver Ihsanullah, industrial/organizational psychologist and SVP of consulting at Linkage, drove the research and led the team that built Linkage's *Advancing Women in Leadership Model™* and corresponding *Advancing Women in Leadership Assessment™*. Jill and her team identified six competencies critical for women's career advancement. They built into the assessment a hidden scale that, along with measuring the six competencies, indicates the potential presence of one or more of the top internal hurdles women face. We are quick to point out that, because internal hurdles impact women differently, they are difficult to measure. However, the data shows that the indicators for all of the hurdles are highly correlated with women's overall assessment scores as well as with other measures of leadership performance. The research provides statistical support for the impact the hurdles can have on women's leadership effectiveness and advancement, whereas the focus of this book is on the proven and practical ways you can run over them, aided by the *stories*—anecdotal evidence—of women leaders. Recent Linkage research, led by Dr. Ihsanullah and Dr. Nada Hashmi from Babson College, demonstrates that the individual hurdles may impact women in specific racial/ethnic groups, as well as in other demographic categories, differentially. These newer findings, which are still in the analysis phase, underline the value of self-assessment on the hurdles.

WHAT DOES THIS MEAN FOR MEN?

It's a confusing time. Frankly, it's not easy being a man these days in a world where women are demanding to be treated equitably in every possible way. If I'm a guy, do I take my female mentee out to lunch alone? Can I hug my female direct report if she's upset?

In 2018, International Women's Day had unprecedented participation globally, with women-led marches or "walk outs" around the world. More and more companies are putting serious time and effort into real strategies to demonstrate the commitment their executives and their organizations have to the equitable treatment and advancement of women.

Whenever there are men in the audience at a talk I'm giving about women's leadership, I'm sure to thank them for being with us and tell them, "I come today in *peace*." (This usually garners some laughter, showing the need to release the tension so inherent in this subject.) If we are to see gender parity and ultimately equal treatment of women everywhere, we need men to co-champion the journey. Setting aside the offenders and the criticality of bringing justice to the women they have harmed, most men I know are trying to figure out how to "be" on the topic of women.

You could say that many are on "high alert" these days, checking to be sure verbal and physical missteps aren't made.

The best progress I have seen is among men and women who are fearlessly examining their thoughts and feelings. This "examination of mindsets" by leaders will no doubt become more prevalent; it will be both encouraged and expected in the workplace. The growth of the unconscious bias training industry alone is proof enough.

Bottom line: Everyone will need to pay close attention to our intentions and our impact as we navigate relationships, especially at work. This requires some interest in self-exploration. Throughout this book, I offer you a snapshot of my journey, which may motivate you to commit to your own. But first, let's look at what these hurdles are about and what you can expect as you read on.

Hurdle #1: The Inner Critic. What's that critical voice in my head? Where is it coming from? Who is it talking about? This is really the mother of all hurdles and the one that is at the heart of the next seven. We will spend time diving deep and untangling the Inner Critic in the next chapter and revisit it in every chapter. The other seven hurdles—*the ones we measure in our Advancing Women in Leadership Assessment*—for you to ponder are as follows:

Hurdle #2: Bias. *What deeply held beliefs do I have that no longer serve me?*

Hurdle #3: Clarity. *Do I know what I want? How can I create a promising future in which I am intentional about my professional advancement?*

Hurdle # 4: Proving my value. *How do I stop doing too much?*

Hurdle # 5: Recognized confidence. *Can I do this?*

Hurdle #6: Branding and presence. *Do others see me as I wish to be seen? Am I showing up in a way that instills confidence in the areas I wish to be known for?*

Hurdle #7: Making the ask. *How do I ask for what I want if it's just for me?*

Hurdle # 8: Building Relationships. *Am I being strategic about developing and leveraging a network of relationships?*

Together, we're going to make this mastery business as simple as it gets. Each chapter is going to cover:

1. The Big Question. What is this particular hurdle asking you that needs an answer?

2. The Big Lie. What might you be telling yourself to stay oblivious?

3. What's possible if you take this hurdle on with intention?

4. How is your Inner Critic tripping you up?

Then, each chapter will offer a more detailed look at the hurdle, including summaries of the research that can help you better understand and share with others what's going on. You'll get lots of practical wisdom about what you need to change to glide over hurdles. And finally, you'll hear the real voices of other women: How They Did It!

It is so important to meet *real women* who unabashedly share not just their accomplishments, but who they are, their values, and the hurdles they've faced. All of the women in the book are committed to practicing self-awareness to change what really matters. They have all faced a hurdle or two (or three or more) and they have all figured out ways to coach their Inner Critic. The stories of these women leaders are second to none; they have developed the skills and ability needed to conquer the hurdle, including the positive impact experienced as a result of taking action. The women featured who gave of their time— and their experience—to be in service to those who read this book are incredible leaders and equally incredible *human beings*. I hope you are touched and inspired by their stories.

Finally, each chapter will offer select tips and suggested activities based on Linkage's successful modular training of thousands of women. When you put it all together, this book is going to:

- Give you the tools and confidence to gain the clarity you need to get more of what you want in life by identifying, managing, and ultimately mastering the hurdles holding you back.

- Motivate you with inspirational stories and practical wisdom from female leaders who have consciously developed the competence and shifts in mindset to overcome specific barriers.

- Re-energize you to engage in the world around you in a more satisfactory way while you're on a journey of self-discovery.

Before we jump in I want to share a personal perspective with you: What I have been personally interested in for years is the role we women have—or can have—in our own and others' career advancement and leadership evolution. While it isn't our job to "fix" the inequities we find ourselves surrounded by in society and the workplace, are there things we can do (or stop doing) that will better facilitate our own professional advancement?

My conclusion is that we women need to get much better at assessing our situations. We need to fearlessly recognize and size up the hurdles to our own advancement and take decisive action. Why? Because once a hurdle becomes visible; once we clear away our limiting self-talk; once we have the experience of successfully gliding over a hurdle despite our imperfections; once that hurdle is named and talked about; once we allow ourselves to share our experience about that hurdle and learn how to "clear it" . . . only then do we begin to see progress for ourselves and are able to help others navigate hurdles, too. We can be intentional as we *glide*.

Let's start hurdling!

CHAPTER 2

STOP THE MADNESS: COACH YOUR CRITIC EVERY STEP OF THE WAY

Hurdle: Inner Critic, the Mother of All Hurdles

The Big Question

Is your Inner Critic stifling your voice, preventing you from making decisions, stopping you from realizing your dreams, hampering your relationships, or minimizing your joy?

The Big Lie

The Inner Critic is my moderate, accurate guiding light.

The Big Opportunity

Reaching your full potential and helping others to reach theirs by clueing in to what's informative and distinguishing limiting beliefs.

The Inner Critic at Work on:

BIAS

One-up: "She is very friendly and nice. I wonder if she's smart."

One-down: "I'm angry at the way I've been treated, but I'll just swallow it. Nobody likes an angry woman."

CLARITY

One-up: "If I didn't need to overcompensate for others, I'd have time to be more strategic about my career."

One-down: "I'm not qualified for what I really want, and no one would support it anyway."

PROVING YOUR VALUE

One-up: "If other people could do things as well as I do them, I wouldn't need to do so much."

One-down: "I am not adding value."

CONFIDENCE

One-up: "They/He/She sucks at . . . "

One-down: "I suck at . . . "

BRANDING AND PRESENCE

One-up: "I don't care what those idiots think of me."

One-down: "I hope I made a good impression despite what I . . . " (*said, didn't say, forgot to say, wore, etc.*)

MAKING THE ASK

One-up: "He is so selfish for taking advantage of me and everyone around him yet again."

One-down: "I won't get what I want anyway, so why bother asking?"

NETWORKING

One-up: "Why would I want to build a relationship/spend time with *her*?"

One-down: "She would never make time for me. Who am I in the scheme of things?"

What You Must Change to Run Over This Hurdle

- Feel the gravity of what "critic" actually means, and access your Compassionate Center to overrun it.

- Notice when you are triggered.

- Pause.

- Channel all the curiosity you can muster.

WHAT ARE WE TALKING ABOUT *REALLY*?

You may ignore it for a little while, but at your most vulnerable times (for instance, when you're feeling stressed, insecure, unhappy, exhausted, or unclear), an inner voice expresses judgment, frustration, or at its most extreme, harshness and contempt. This "inner voice" can be instructive, and clue us into some feelings or thoughts that might be helpful as we navigate life and relationships. When extreme, this inner voice can also hurl offensive assaults on us and others. Despite where the Inner Critic is aimed, the commentary is anything but happy, loving, compassionate, and curious.

WHAT IS AN INNER CRITIC?

For me, it's that voice inside my head that is critical of myself *and* critical of others. The Inner Critic can be instructive. If we find a person or situation that irritates us, it is most likely for good reason. When we have that initial judgmental thought, chances are there is a person or situation that isn't quite right. Something is off. We have a moment—even a flash—of helpful "say what?"

But when the Inner Critic lingers, harps every day, and becomes increasingly harsh, its utility, I would argue, has passed and that voice needs to take a *time-out*. Busy, well-intended working women need a debilitating voice in their head about as much as they need to be jumping 3.5 feet in the air at a moment's notice (the average height of a high running hurdle).

When we catch ourselves being self-critical, we need to practice abundant self-compassion. When we catch ourselves being critical of others, we need to practice compassion and get exquisitely curious about them and/or the situation. It's that easy and that hard.

So what are some examples of the physical, emotional, and mental characteristics, actions (or lack of), or daily decisions your Inner Critic may berate you for and trip you up on? The Inner Critic has the power to latch onto what could begin as a miniscule insecurity and enlarge it to a size that shatters your self-esteem and destroys your opportunities for advancement— if you let it. The seven other hurdles we'll be exploring in this book can serve as the symptoms and the early warning alarms that signal the ferocity of your Inner Critic. *But it's equally true that your Inner Critic can make you blind to the other hurdles and incapable of gliding.* Essentially, you have to pay equal attention to these hurdles to increase your chances of mastering your Inner Critic. And you have to learn to coach and redirect your Inner Critic so you can glide over the other hurdles.

There is no way I could recognize (much less glide over) any hurdle if I didn't learn how to bring myself back to a place in my mind of knowing that I am worthy, whole, and complete *no matter what.* I spent most of my formative years *appearing* self-confident and friendly, and *feeling on the inside* desperately not good enough.

Most of my "not good enoughs" were localized in body image issues. At 5'9 in 6th grade I was too big, too tall, wore glasses, and nothing seemed to fit me. *I* didn't seem to fit me, and more often than not, I felt uncomfortable in my skin. Especially around girls that were more petite, more fit, thinner, and perfect-sighted. I stood out in ways I never asked for. I felt different, and thus, had a well-honed Inner Critic at a very early age, ready to remind me how totally different—and not good enough—I was at a moment's notice. It was only a bit later in life, when I gained some self-confidence in my abilities to lead and get stuff done, that I (unconsciously) developed that not-so-nice, often unspoken aspect of the Inner Critic: pointing that judgmental and critical voice in my mind *at those around me*.

The only thing that could derail me from being blissfully unaware of my impact on others (especially when I felt I knew better than them) was when I caught sight of my image in a mirror which would cue the blaring and well-used tapes to play body-hating self-talk. Too big. Too much. *Yuck.*

I was first introduced to the impact of these mean voices on me and my relationships while working alongside bestselling author and nationally-acclaimed psychotherapist, Terry Real. As managing director and then president and CEO of Terry's Relational Life Institute, I had the good fortune of attending hundreds of hours of trainings offered to certify mental health professionals in a methodology for counseling couples, and to equip couples themselves. The Institute also held relationship boot camps for couples, offering tools to better manage their most intimate relationships.

As with many useful conceptual frameworks aimed at changing behavior, managing relationships starts with *us*. I learned from Terry to cast aside the all too familiar (and arguably easier) pattern of analyzing others, and to begin with better managing my own thoughts and feelings. Job No. 1 was to notice what I came to lovingly call my Inner Critic, and how she wreaks havoc in my life.

What I learned from Terry and many of his seasoned and exceptional student-turned-teaching therapists was this: I don't have to be in so much emotional pain about how I am *not good enough*. My relationships can be easier. I can navigate conflict with more ease and less stress. I can have a practice all my own that will leave me feeling worthy in any environment I am in and sensitive to the unique value others bring. What has evolved for me since being introduced to these concepts is a moment-to-moment practice of *returning* to a place of 1) feeling worthy, whole, and complete (compassion for self) when I am introduced to all the ways I am imperfect, and 2) curiosity and compassion for that person/s who I find myself being critical of.

I want to emphasize that this is a practice where we *return* to a place of compassion and curiosity (a place I call "Compassionate Center") because, as a human who is in relationships with other humans, I am bound to get triggered.

WHEN YOUR INNER CRITIC IS DIRECTED AT OTHERS

You may find that when your Inner Critic is directed, not at your own shortcomings and imperfections, but at another, it is usually because you are communicating with someone who (for you) is showing up as a know-it-all (*what a jerk!*), or lacking in curiosity (*such an idiot*), or as arrogant and thus unaware of their impact (*total monster!*). Rarely will you say these things out loud. However, let's not confuse your expression of these thoughts with the level others *feel or sense* from your unspoken, non-verbal, maybe even self-righteous contempt.

Here is one of the magic bullets about managing the Inner Critic when its wrath is pointed at someone other than you:

You can't be simultaneously peering down your nose at someone in an internal swirl of "what an idiot," and be genuinely curious about that person or the situation you find yourself in.

So, you need to build an internal mechanism to notice the feelings (anger, annoyance, disgust), then notice the thoughts (jerk, idiot, monster), and then push *pause*. Once you pause your own thinking, you then can consciously switch to thinking with curiosity. For example, let's say you are confronted with someone who is angry or overly emotional and you are annoyed. Instead of brushing them off or acting in kind, a shift to curiosity would include first *noticing that you are annoyed and pausing that feeling long enough to get curious.* "I wonder what's making him so angry? Is this how she is typically, or is there something triggering this behavior?"

For practice with the routine of inquiry, check out the work of the Inquiry Institute. Founder Marilee Adams, PhD, coined the concept of QUESTION THINKING™, created using brain-based knowledge about the importance of questions in thinking and communication. Besides compassion, curiosity is the most powerful opponent of the Inner Critic.

WHEN YOUR INNER CRITIC IS DIRECTED AT YOU

Triggers that fire up my nastiest Inner Critic are when I realize I might have come across with a tone I didn't intend *(you're so intense, Susan!)*, when I say something that I wish I had framed differently *(think more carefully before you speak!)*, or at the moments that I see the discrepancy between what I teach and what I catch myself doing *(you're not very good at this either, huh? Who are you to teach this work?)*.

I dressed up as my Inner Critic for our Halloween work party a few years back. My hair was in a very tight bun. I was dressed very conservatively in a high-collar shirt, tweed blazer, and pearls. I had small glasses on which were resting at the tip of my nose. The only posture this physical manifestation of my Inner Critic needed to make was (with pursed lips and an expression of scrutiny) one hand on the hip and the other hand lifted up (as if in your face) with the index finger poised to take you down. That's my girl! She can get cruel. And she's *really* good at her job.

In their book, *How Women Rise: Break the 12 Habits Holding You Back From Your Next Raise, Promotion, or Job*, Sally Helgesen and Marshall Goldsmith posit that forgiveness and self-forgiveness are the most powerful tools they know for women with a tendency to judge or second guess themselves. I would add that forgiveness of self and others on an ongoing, sometimes moment-to-moment basis, is essential if we wish to manifest the life we women want and realize our full potential.

It is imperative to at least think seriously about your Inner Critic and how frequent it may get in the way of your life quality, personally and professionally, as it assaults your sense of self-worth and your sense of the worthiness of others. Coaching your Inner Critic is vital to your success as you scale each of the hurdles in the coming chapters. As you take risks and try on new ways of thinking and acting, you will need an internal "muscle" of personal power and centeredness. When you stop the madness of this sabotaging self-talk and replace it with compassion and curiosity, you liberate yourself and those in your sphere in ways that will be life-changing. It's really hard to make a change and/or come to accept something (really, genuinely accept— even embrace—the possibility of a person or situation) if your Inner Critic is leading the way.

Imagine a day where you felt good in your skin more often than not; where you had less conflict with others; where you weren't so exhausted from trying so hard; where you weren't accepting things you shouldn't; where you had people tell you that something about you seems . . . more open, somehow happier, less "wound up," *different*? What would be possible?

Imagine a day when, instead of feeling insecure and making yourself small and giving up, turning to the outside world for affirmation by way of acceptance from another, acquisition of a material item, or gratification from an accomplishment (which are all arguably positive yet fleeting alternatives), you *paused* in your vulnerable moment and breathed in some compassion for yourself, reminding yourself that you are *enough and worthy* right this very minute, and it felt *real and good*? What would be possible?

Imagine a day when, instead of shutting out those who disappoint and anger you (doing what you want anyway despite the impact on others), or lashing out and giving yourself permission to express contempt (demanding things be done your way despite the impact on others), you *paused* in your self-righteous "I'm right/they're stupid" moment and breathed in some compassion for others, reminding yourself that they are worthy as human beings to be treated with respect and curiosity? What would be possible?

MASTERING THE INNER CRITIC:
A PERSONAL JOURNEY

Before I ever even considered writing this book I often shared with others the role my own Inner Critic has played in my life and the simple (yet challenging!) practice of coaching those distracting—often harsh, always judgmental—voices in my head. The Cliff Notes version is that my life has been a near-perfect-how-to design of events for honing a very over-eager Inner Critic—and producing an abundance of hurdles. Yet these same life events have also given me the will to master my Inner Critic and the courage and support to learn how to glide. Let me explain.

I relate to the story *The Jungle Book*—only instead of a little boy being raised by a family of wolves, I was a little girl raised by men. At a very young age, I wasn't a "tomboy" nor was I a "girly-girl." I didn't fit any stereotype; I didn't think at all about my girl-ness. The thing I share in common with Mowgli is that I belonged in the world in which I was raised because I was accepted and loved and encouraged.

This sense of belonging came at a time when I wasn't fully aware (but would be in years to come) of my awkwardness. Not only was I a little girl who was being raised by a single father, I had curly, red hair cut short like Little Orphan Annie, Flintstones-brand eye glasses (which, for a time, covered up an eye patch over my right eye in an effort to strengthen my left), and pants and shirts that were just a stitch too short on my taller-than-average, little-girl frame.

Feeling the discomfort of being different as a kid was mostly neutralized by the love I felt from my father. He was funny, loving, warm-hearted, attentive, encouraging, and had a gift with words. He did what millions of women (and a few men, too) have done: He took on the sole responsibility of running a household, providing income, and caring for children. Dad never set out to raise two kids as a single father. He did eventually find a new life partner in my step-mother, Maria, but that wasn't until I was an early teen. Until he had Maria's support, Dad managed it all, and did so with an abundance of love. My parents had divorced when I was 3, and my brother and I stayed on the small New England island where we lived with our dad. Our mother moved off island and out of state where we visited with her several times a year. It wasn't ideal, but I had the benefit of learning from two very different worlds: my on-island world with my single dad and small community, and my off-island world where my mom and her side of the family introduced me to New York City, Broadway shows, and the world of business.

My stepfather, David, married my mom when I was 8. He worked in New York City for a big publishing company where he was ad director and then publisher of a major magazine. It was in late middle school when he invited me to join him for a day in the office. I recall this experience like it was yesterday. The hustle of the city was thrilling to me. The high-rise where his office was located was in the heart of Midtown Manhattan, and it felt like everything important happened within a block radius. The foods, smells, people, and speed—electric! But what I recall most is walking in with him and being greeted by a very nice woman who sat outside his office. She took his coat, got him coffee, and handed him his agenda for the day. He was friendly and appreciative (an extrovert's extrovert). He had a corner office, and his furniture and walls were littered with beautiful knick-knacks and paintings.

I recall thinking how lucky David was to have someone help him organize his world. My mom was a personal secretary for an insurance agent back in the Connecticut suburbs, and every so often, I would go to work with her and help with filing or mailings. I had seen office life before, and my genuine appreciation for those in "support functions" is real—likely because I saw how things functioned *because* of those like my mom, who helped organize everything. But this world of David's opened my eyes to the "other side," and before I knew it, my awe was reinforced with his words that day: "Honey, you can do this, too, someday you know." The combined encouragement from all of my parents made me feel confident that I could do anything I set my mind to.

Somehow, this "I can do it" tween morphed into a very active yet insecure high schooler, an overachieving college student, and a very driven young professional who, when she wasn't being a competitive workhorse, was wracked with self-doubt. Who was this monster Inner Critic and where did she come from? And what on earth could I do to remove her stunning power over me? It turned out I had access to the remedy within me, I just didn't know it. You do too. Enter compassion.

ACCESSING YOUR COMPASSIONATE CENTER

You think "accessing a Compassionate Center" sounds a little hokey and new-age-therapeutic? Stay with me. At its core, compassion is the desire to relieve suffering. If you feel stressed, frustrated, unsafe, unproductive, or indecisive that is, indeed, some measure of suffering. The scale could be miniscule or mammoth. You don't need to create the Compassionate Center; you just need to access it. In the interest of the premise of the seven other hurdles (and their mother!), your Compassionate Center is the place you dwell where you fully understand that you are okay, worthy, enough right now. This is the place where you deeply believe you are no better or worse than another human being. Accessing your Compassionate Center is believing that there isn't anything out there in the world (a person who will love you, a material item that will delight you, or an accomplishment that will gratify you) that will make you more worthy than you are right now (as you read this). There is no language you will speak, there is no salary you will make, there is no house or town in which you will live, there is no lover you will find, there is no mountain you will climb that will make you more worthy as a human being—and thus, *more* okay—than you are this very minute. The belief you must cast aside is that your worthiness (your "okay-ness") will be found *outside of yourself*.

Does it feel awesome to be loved and accepted? Oh, yes! Is life easier to afford when we make more money? Yes! Does it feel great to learn a skill and master it? For sure. Is it rewarding to be offered a promotion? I believe it is. Is it awesome to set a goal and accomplish it? Uh-huh. Yet the big lie you tell yourself is that these things will result in your lasting peace and happiness. That when you XYZ (fill in the blank), *then* you will be enough. As if there is an arrival at this thing called "worthiness." So, you buy the beautiful things. You seek to be loved and accepted and win over others. You achieve bigger and harder goals. Only to want . . . more. Only to feel like perhaps the *next* brand-name handbag (or designer suit, luxury car, bigger house) will make you feel the way you want, the *next* person who accepts or loves you will fill that hole inside you, or when you reach the *next* goal (title, role, level of leadership responsibility) you'll finally be satisfied.

I'm sorry to be the bearer of bad news. The "if only I XYZ" strategy of worthiness is not a winning strategy. Trust me. I have tried it all on for size and it doesn't work. I have witnessed others buy or hustle for their worthiness too. It doesn't work because there is no permanent arrival to this place called worthiness. While an entire chapter is devoted to the topic of confidence, it's important to note that worthiness is different than confidence. But the two get confused. Worthiness you *believe*. Confidence you *build*. Think about it: if you want to more confidently speak a third language, the best way to go about it is to study and practice speaking the language. As a result of your effort, your fluency will likely improve, resulting in your increased confidence when speaking that language. This results not in your being better than others generally, but in you being perhaps better at speaking the language. Where there is confusion between confidence and worthiness is believing that when you speak that third language more fluently, you will be a better human being—

somehow more worthy and thus better than others as a result of your newfound skills. In actuality, this is a false sense of worthiness. Why? What happens if you can't conjure up the right word, in a high-stakes moment or in your third language? How do you feel now? You may be able to speak the language better than many others and as such have increased confidence speaking that language, but you won't be better than them, and this doesn't change your worthiness as a human being—or theirs. You were worthy before you learned any of the languages you speak; they are worthy too.

Let's play this out: You're overseas attending a global conference and find yourself making small talk at a reception. What a great opportunity to speak in your newly-minted third language. You ask in that tongue if anyone speaks the language and your question is received with some blank stares. Then one person replies, "I can speak so-so, not well." You then probe further, in the third language, and find that in fact, you are SO MUCH BETTER than this other person. You feel triumphant. Holy cow! Doesn't she LIVE in the country that considers this language their first language? Aren't you the bomb for being the one with fluency in three languages! Ha-hah! You feel your shoulders swing back, your chin lift up, you are best.

A few more people enter the room, and overhear you speaking the language. They dive in with speed and delight and you find yourself utterly lost in the exchange, unable to keep up with their accent and speed of delivery. You feel about an inch high. You thought you improved so much more than you actually did. These people are so much more fluent than you are. You are embarrassed about being puffed up, feeling better than others, only moments earlier. You find your shoulders have dropped a bit and you look for a reason to exit. The external locus of control that is in charge of your worthiness (in this example, speaking a language) is designed perfectly to inflate or deflate your belief in yourself and in others.

You might be thinking, "Wait—isn't this perfect? Life *should* lift us up and knock us down. Isn't that how we learn resilience and agility and humility?" Well, not exactly. The difference between a life lesson (becoming aware that we are human and thus imperfect) and how we get there (extreme thoughts of being superior or inferior) is the challenge. In my experience working with women in particular, the "extreme" nature of moving from feeling better than another to feeling not good enough is what causes them and the people around them pain. Men have Inner Critics, yes, but women want (and need) to name it, discuss it, and coach it. Feedback from thousands of women has confirmed for me that the Inner Critic is more acute for women (often wreaking havoc in our lives), given the hurdles we have to surmount. This is why accessing the Compassionate Center, and taking action from that place is so critical.

Picture your Compassionate Center as a place inside of you that you can conjure up whenever need be and return to when you need to. It's a place of forgiveness, empathy, compassion, and humor. Just thinking of it reminds you to be gentle with whatever you're contending with. Your Compassionate Center is the part of you that takes a child in her arms whispering "it's okay" and "I'm right here for you" when they are crying after falling off their bike. At its core, it is love. It is acceptance. It is where safety is created. If Compassionate Center had a slogan on a T-shirt, it would say, "You are enough and you so very much matter."

By not having honed access to your Compassionate Center, you may have looked for your worthiness everywhere but there. The good news is that the muscle of your Compassionate Center, and thus the core ingredient to the practice of mastering your Inner Critic, has been there all along. You just have to get to know it and use it. If you are an adult, it is not the job of your father or mother or partner or colleague or daughter or friend to bring you back to feeling worthy. It helps if you have people who believe in you and encourage you to take action. However, if you tap into the part of you that can tell yourself you are worthy, whole, complete, right here, right now before looking for that elsewhere and setting yourself up for potential disappointment when other people and things don't suffice, why wouldn't you?

My goal is to mindfully be in Compassionate Center with myself and others as often as humanly possible. This is a choice, a practice which has become a habit. It is rooted in goodwill, in generosity, and in abundance. The moments when I live and lead from Compassionate Center look like this: I am open hearted to myself and trust that I bring something of worth to the situation/conversation. I am aware that I am no better or worse, fundamentally and as a human being, than whomever I am connecting with. (This includes both the multi-millionaire CEO of a several-billion dollar enterprise and the garage attendant with whom I left my car.) I am respectful and open-hearted to others and trust they bring something of worth to the situation/conversation. I am looking for connection points. I am thinking in questions, seeking to learn and grow. There is an abundance of appreciation for others and also for me and my own gifts and talents. I consciously experience gratitude, and find myself feeling thankful. When I am living and leading from this place, I deeply accept my awesomeness in the world and I deeply assume the awesomeness of others. I am aware that we are all human, and as such, utterly imperfect. I am no less awesome, or imperfect, as a human being than anyone else. This, you could say, is my "happy place." And it is available to me anytime I want. You can have one, too.

But let's be honest, life doesn't always allow us to be kicking around in the "happy place" of Compassionate Center, does it? We get triggered, because we are confronted with evidence that we are, in fact, imperfect (not enough in a specific situation) or we are confronted with feelings of disappointment, or even anger, about someone else being imperfect (not enough in a specific situation). This is where the madness begins. Let's say it's been 18 months since you first raised the case for a promotion. You've been turned down due to a "salary freeze" or an "average performance review." You know you're already performing the duties that this upgraded position entails, and you've had 18 months to practice the duties and document the results you garnered; you need the title, accolades, and raise to make it official. In the corporate world, this is both a common spot to be in and one that the Inner Critic loves to swim and splash in. "Why ask again since you're obviously inadequate?" "Stay safe; at least you have a steady paycheck!" "They'll find another reason to decline, so don't bother." "That other fool is just waiting to sink his teeth into the title."

If you think that this negative self-talk is not madness, consider this: The Inner Critic feeds off of negativity, insecurity, isolation, stagnancy, and misery. At its strongest, it makes you more miserable because you're losing out on precious time and experiences—the fruits of life.

Action: Envision your Compassionate Center somewhere in your body. I think of mine where my bellybutton is because it is the center of my body. Feeling my diaphragm move when I inhale the thought of that Compassionate Center and exhale the madness of the Inner Critic helps me to physically center. If your heart area is a better place for you to think your "center" lives, great. I like to hold my hand literally over that space at times and take a few deep breaths. It helps to bring me back there.

NOTICING WHEN
YOU'RE TRIGGERED

Trigger scenario #1: You are thinking about this crazy-sounding place of bliss called Compassionate Center, and your thoughts are interrupted by an incoming call. You look down and see it is your manager. You pick up. He asks, "Did you get those slides done for the board presentation yet?" You immediately check the schedule, confirming they aren't due to him for another three business days. In this moment, you want to SCREAM. Your Inner Critic just took command and is furious at him, and you find yourself thinking: "Seriously? Is he going to pull this again—where he acts like I'm late on a deliverable when I'm not? He just wants to cover his ass. He sucks."

Trigger scenario #2: You are thinking about this crazy-sounding place of bliss called Compassionate Center, and your thoughts are interrupted by an incoming call. You look down and see it is your manager. You pick up. He asks, "Did you get those slides done for the board presentation yet?" You immediately assume you have missed the deadline and that you messed up. In this moment, you want to SCREAM. Your Inner Critic just took command and is furious at you: "Seriously? Can you manage to do anything right and on time? Way to win over the boss and show him how much value you bring. You suck."

Noticing when you're triggered is not that hard. In fact, you likely have been triggered in the last twenty-four hours. If you live with children, potentially a few times. Being triggered, in the domain of Inner Critic mastery, is when you find yourself either in an active reaction or you find yourself ruminating about how you suck or another person sucks. It's the same voice and energy, just pointing in different directions. The trigger is fueled by harshness, contempt, criticism, or feelings of annoyance. When you are triggered, disgust rises. When this energy is pointed at you, the aim is to (sometimes with excruciating detail) berate yourself about how you "shouldn't have," "should have," "were supposed to," and any other active nastiness you can dish out about the level to which *you* suck.

When this energy is pointed not at you but at others, the aim is to (sometimes with excruciating detail) berate others about how they "shouldn't have," "should have," "were supposed to," and any other active nastiness you can dish out about the level to which *they* suck. Most workplaces these days value being a "great place to work" and won't tolerate bullying behavior.

I want to acknowledge that the Inner Critic isn't always "inner." It does turn "outer." Let's stay focused on what we think and feel, knowing that this will eventually (or quickly) impact what we say and do. When we slow down and first become aware of what we think and feel, what we say and do is far more intentional and productive.

Your Inner Critic voice is how you know if you are triggered. Who and how you get triggered depends on you, your life experiences, your chosen attitude, your beliefs, your education, your expectations, your disappointments, your moments of pride, and your own "filters."

To be triggered is to be human. People will make you angry. You will miss the mark. People will make mistakes. You will make mistakes. It's all normal and comes with the territory of being human. However, how you think and feel when you are triggered, what you give yourself permission to say and do, and the actions that you take in those moments where generosity is decidedly lacking, is what self-mastery is all about. The consequences of how we manage ourselves is the business case for self-awareness. The aim: Return authentically to Compassionate Center as quickly as humanly possible and lead your life powerfully from that place.

In his 1995 bestseller, *Emotional Intelligence*, Daniel Goleman popularized "EQ" and the crucial skills needed to master it. Why? He suggested by mastering EQ, our success in relationships, work, and even physical well-being would be positively impacted. In the book, the power of the amygdala, the part of our brain that handles emotions, is reviewed. The amygdala can get triggered with an immediate and overwhelming emotional response out of proportion to the stimulus at hand. Since this seminal work, many in the fields of psychology, neuroscience, and behavioral economics have added incredibly to our understanding of the human mind, and how we can manage our bodies so our brain is high-functioning (as Dr. Tara Swart suggests in Chapter 4 on the hurdle of Clarity). What hasn't changed since the discovery of the amygdala in early 1820s, is that this part of our brain handles emotions, and we as humans, run the risk of our emotions overpowering our sensibility in the moment. Most of the time, we know not to express certain emotions, but sometimes, we literally can't help it; we get "hijacked" in the moment. This does not excuse us from having to take responsibility for the impact of our reactivity. It does, however, prove that you aren't crazy. Getting triggered as we navigate through our day is part of how we're wired.

I raise the activity of the brain when triggered because, depending upon the situation and how triggered you are, you will want to have a range of options when it comes to how and for how long you practice pausing.

PAUSING

You know now what Compassionate Center is. You know now that it's almost impossible to stay there 24/7/365 because life happens and you will be triggered. Now what, you ask? It isn't any more or less complicated than taking a pause to *return* to your Compassionate Center. When you notice your Inner Critic is in control, pausing simply means you push pause. First, you need to notice the Inner Critic at work, then you need to PAUSE her. The more triggered you are, the longer your pause will need to be. If you're full-on swept up in a reactive hijack, your brain needs time to calm down. Take a walk. Get it out in a journal. Sit with it and do nothing but breathe.

Pausing When Your Inner Critic Goes After You

Do not seek out another until you have paused and returned to Compassionate Center. Here's why: If you are triggered into a place of hell where you are the worst (mother, employee, manager, wife, partner, sister, friend, daughter, etc. . . .) on the planet, chances are you are experiencing shame. This is a great time to seek out someone who adores you so they can tell you what you want to hear, right? Not so fast. Of course leaning on others to remind you of your awesomeness is a great way to come back to Compassionate Center from your self-berating walk down the hall of shame. That said, this is the moment when you can practice flexing the muscle of pausing. Resist the urge to *do* anything. Tune into the most compassionate part of you, the one who is finding little you just skinned her knee and is in need of big love. That's the purpose of the pause. To breathe and return to a place of compassion. Take a page out of my mantra if need be, and call yourself "honey." As in "oh, honey. You try so darn hard and you are so perfectly imperfect. You have gifts and talents galore, and like everyone, you are not above and beyond learning. It's okay. You are okay. This will be okay." It might even make you laugh, all this sweet talking you'll be doing with yourself. I laugh at myself all the time.

This self-forgiving talk I give myself isn't the same as being off the hook for repairing with another if need be. It's just the first step so that when you take responsibility for your imperfection/miss/mistake/unintended impact, you can be sure you do so from Compassionate Center. If you don't take this step, you might be at risk of apologizing over and over for your mishap, or ducking and hiding in the halls of shame and never taking responsibility for yourself, or running around in desperation to everyone you know looking for affirmation and confirmation that you don't suck *that bad.* These options, while familiar, will take more time and often won't result in you *really* feeling any better. Instead, you have access to an awesome coach who is at your disposal every hour of every day. Use her.

Pausing When Your Inner Critic Goes After Someone Else

Do not seek out another when you are frustrated with them until you have paused and returned to Compassionate Center. Here's why: If you are triggered into a place of self-righteous indignation where the person you have been triggered by might be the worst (mother, employee, manager, wife, partner, sister, friend, daughter, etc. . . .) on the planet, chances are you are experiencing grandiosity. You don't feel harshness toward yourself; you feel disgusted or in judgment of another. If you choose to confront this person while your Inner Critic is in command, I promise you that it won't go well. If you do take action in the reactivity of your triggered feelings, you will run the risk of coming across (even if you try really hard not to) as patronizing, condescending, or downright insulting. This runs the risk of inviting three knee-jerk possible reactions from the other party: They will argue with you about the merits of their side (fight), they will want to run away from you because you're being mean and/or they don't like conflict (flight), or they will feel compelled to fix the situation, likely before fully hearing you out or perhaps before you have had time and space to get clear about what you need to make the situation better for you (fix). Instead, if you take pause before you seek out the person until your state of fury has mostly passed, chances are you'll have a more productive conversation.

The work to do when you're triggered by someone else and you think they are the problem is no different than the work suggested when you are triggered into the halls of shame. Take pause and actively think with compassion about the other. (I can hear you say, "What? Are you kidding me? Why on earth would I be compassionate when they are such a jerk?") Any activity in this book is, first and foremost, for you and your own sanity and second, to narrow the gap between your intention and impact with others. The reason you take this getting-off-your-high-horse business seriously is because it can change your life and relationships for the better. The work to be done when you notice your Inner Critic going off on another is to first pause and say, "Huh. That wasn't a very nice thing to think." Is there something I might be missing? Is there something about the other person that I relate to? Is there something that I could learn from this person or situation? Could I confront the situation with greater levels of curiosity? Here's a little secret: you can't be genuinely curious and indignant at the same time. Compassionate Center is fueled by love and curiosity. Taking the pause simply means giving yourself the space and time to get there.

Upon hearing about the two-way street of the Inner Critic (she is *so not* just here to judge and criticize *you*, everyone is fair game for her), many people wonder, "Well, what if the other person is wrong, what if I'm right and they are XYZ (arrogant, stupid, an idiot, incompetent, a control freak, a maniacal perfectionist, a liar, etc.)?" My reply to this is: So, what if they are? Are you giving yourself permission to think and behave in ways that elevate you into a place of being "better than" this person? If so, it's for sure a losing strategy. Don't confuse human BEINGS for human RESOURCES. There are a lot of good human beings who are the wrong resource for the job. Be careful here. Don't confuse the two. Think about how you would want to be treated if your judgment or behavior was in question: You would likely prefer to be treated from a place of curiosity and a sprinkle of benefit of the doubt. I have caught myself thinking a critical thought of another and have pushed pause and asked myself: Are you needing to be right, or are you concerned about how they are seeing or thinking about the situation? So often, I need to reflect on that. As I have disclosed in Chapter 5, I like things done my way. So my "good judgement" can in fact be a bit of covert desire to do it my way instead. When doing it my way isn't the issue (because the same end will be reached should different paths be taken) and I find myself concerned with something someone did or said, I need to quickly get curious about why. My Inner Critic tips me off. She is useful that way.

And then I ask her (ever-so-politely) to sit the hell down. My Compassionate Center is beckoning, and my first order of business is to take pause.

CHANNELING ALL THE COMPASSION AND CURIOSITY YOU CAN MUSTER

I feel compelled to share a truth I learned over and over from several brilliant clinicians with whom I worked while at Terry Real's Relational Life Institute. Our shame causes us pain. We are more motivated to get to Compassionate Center from a place of feeling not good enough because it hurts to feel not good enough. We are more likely to try on calling our self "honey" than lingering in the depths of our *not-good-enoughs* for a moment longer. On the other hand, our self-righteous indignation (implicit or explicit) feels good to us (who doesn't like being right?) and hurts others around us. Thus, we are likely less motivated to push pause and seek Compassionate Center when the person who is the jerk (or the utterly incompetent one) is someone else. This creates a dilemma where we run the risk of not being as intrinsically motivated to stop the madness of the Inner Critic when she's on fire about the idiots around her.

This is the most important part of this book. If you get nothing else, get this: your power to lead in your life and at work will multiply and magnify when you lead *yourself* from Compassionate Center. Your power rests in your own capacity to return to Compassionate Center with swiftness and intention. No one wants to be around someone who overtly or covertly exudes that they think they are better than others around them. I'm not talking about confidence. I'm talking about arrogance and the belief that you are better than another. If you lead from a place of thinking you know it all and others are idiots, you will eventually be that leader who is having to walk alone. No followers. People will leave you at work and at home. (Either forever or in the moment, mentally or physically.) Don't give yourself permission to be a know-it-all jerk. Just don't. If you are triggered regularly by the same person or situation into feelings of annoyance or disgust, here are my questions for you: What is not okay for you about this person or situation? Get specific. What do you want to see change? What do you need from that person or situation to engage fully and in a spirit of abundance? Take this seriously. Senior leaders derail most often because they can't manage themselves and their relationships, not because of technical incompetence or a shortage of IQ. The first relationship we need to manage is the one with ourselves, beginning with the understanding that what we think and feel drives what we say and do. If you take action (speak, complain, make a request, and seek to repair) in the absence of compassion and curiosity for yourself and the other, please understand this will continue the unnecessary cycle of blame and shame. Instead, take pause. Do whatever it takes to return to your Compassionate Center.

Bringing yourself back to a place in your mind of knowing that you are worthy, whole, complete *no matter what* will help you courageously scale the hurdles. As discussed in our chapter on Recognized Confidence (Chapter 6), all the self-talk in the world won't help you scale. You need to take action. You need to *Just Do It*. Where coaching the Inner Critic can help is having a dialogue with yourself rooted in Compassionate Center as you take risks and take courageous action.

You don't have to be in so much emotional pain about how you are *not good enough*. Your relationships can be easier. You can navigate conflict with more ease and less stress. You can have a practice all your own that will leave you feeling worthy in any environment you are in, and sensitive to the unique value others bring. What can evolve for you is a moment-to-moment practice of *returning* to a place of 1) feeling worthy, whole, and complete (compassion for self) when you are confronted with your imperfections, and 2) curiosity and compassion for that person who you find yourself being critical of. The one you have been waiting for is you.

Forgiveness of self and others on an ongoing, sometimes moment-to-moment basis is essential if you wish to manifest the life you want and realize your full potential. Take it a moment at a time, make the return to center more and more frequent. Breathe in compassion. Breathe in forgiveness. Breathe in curiosity. Laugh out imperfection. And from Compassionate Center, let's look at these other hidden hurdles, shall we?

CHAPTER 3

WHAT ABOUT BIAS?

Hurdle: Bias

The Big Question

What deeply held beliefs do I have that no longer serve me?

The Big Lie

Staying blissfully unaware of biases won't have negative consequences on my ability to be a high-impact leader or my ability to advance. I can handle it.

The Big Opportunity

Your formation and readiness as a leader will accelerate if you have awareness and continued curiosity about common biases and your own biases.

The Inner Critic at Work on Bias

One-up: "She is very friendly and nice. I wonder if she's smart . . ."

One-down: "I'm angry at the way I've been treated, but I'll just swallow it. Nobody likes an angry woman."

> ### What You Must Change to Run Over This Hurdle
>
> Identify and become aware of your own unconscious biases about yourself and others, and how others' biases may be impacting you.
>
> ———————
>
> *Remember: Everyone believes others are more biased than they are.*
>
> ———————

I want to start with a passionate plea: PLEASE PAY ATTENTION!

This is the hurdle that at first seems so insignificant that we don't even see it until it's too late. And either as a victim—or perpetrator—we can't glide.

Sometimes a bias is used against us. ("Financial analysts just aren't good with creative tasks.") Sometimes we're using a bias as our own default rationale for a decision. ("She's not ready for the promotion. Her strength is managing teams, not running a business.") Sometimes we use an implicit bias to fuel our own Inner Critic. ("Hey. I'm an introvert. I'm not ever going to be good at schmoozing.")

It's also possible that we sometimes speak up and name the bias or catch ourselves using one. But mostly this bias stuff is subtle and nuanced and complex. A tiny, almost imperceptible drip, drip, drip. Which is what makes it toxic and dangerous. If you're following today's debates, conversations, protests, and even law suits about race and gender you have probably run across the term "microaggression" or "micro-inequities." These aren't the big, blatant headline-worthy name-calling events. These are the day-to-day casual remarks or even unspoken "attitudes" that over time take root. Like mastering our Inner Critic, this hurdle requires our thoughtful and moment-to-moment attention.

WHAT ARE WE TALKING ABOUT *REALLY*?

Here's the low-down on stereotypes, bias, and unconscious bias: **Stereotypes** are beliefs about people based on their membership in a group, such as race, gender, nationality, religion, sexual orientation, education, etc. (Often, stereotypes are unnoticed automatic thoughts and beliefs.) **Bias** is positive or negative treatment of people based on their membership in a group. Bias is usually the result of a cognitive shortcut, often growing out of stereotypes. It manifests in inequitable judgment, unfair acts, and systematic barriers. **Implicit (or Unconscious) Bias** is positive or negative treatment of people that is unnoticed by the actor.

The Cambridge English Dictionary has what I find to be the strongest definition of bias: *The action of supporting or opposing a particular person or thing in an unfair way, because of allowing personal opinions to influence your judgment.* The last part is the most important part: "allowing personal opinions to influence your judgement." (If you are thinking, *Of course my personal opinions influence my judgement, Susan!*, stay with me and read on.)

We have established that we all have biases, known (*conscious*) and unknown (*unconscious*). Examples of some of the often unconscious biases that impact the workplace include:

- **Affinity Bias:** The tendency to warm up to people like ourselves.

- **Perception Bias:** The tendency to form stereotypes and assumptions about certain groups that make it impossible to make an objective judgment about members of those groups.

- **Halo Effect, or Optimism Bias:** The tendency to think everything about a person is good because you like that person.

- **Anchoring and Insufficient Adjustment Bias:** The tendency to be over-reliant on the first piece of information you hear.

- **Confirmation Bias:** The tendency for people to seek information that confirms pre-existing beliefs or assumptions.

- **Group Think:** The tendency to drive for consensus with others at the cost of a realistic appraisal of alternatives.

- **Recency:** The tendency to weight the latest information more heavily than older data.

Our implicit ways of processing information impact our attitudes and decisions—*without us being aware*. If you aren't already thinking about the plausible negative consequences of the short list above as you navigate at work, let me be very clear: all these different types of biases are happening whether you are aware of them or not. With perception bias, for example, we habitually assume things about people born and raised in certain countries and regions, and judge people by their appearance. We may not do it on purpose, but the majority of us are guilty of some amount of judgment. Our ultimate moment-to-moment practice is to lead with *conscious awareness* (the mental state that will be pressed upon throughout our work with the hurdles), ultimately shifting from a state of unconsciousness (resulting in exclusion of others) to a state of conscious awareness (where we can consciously include or accept those who we don't automatically relate to). I know, I know. Being oblivious can have its upside.

The more I attune to my own unintended impact and/or catch myself in a biased thought, I can't help but agree that ignorance sometimes is bliss. (Cue the Inner Critic: *Did you REALLY just have that thought, you horrible, mean woman who professes to be self-aware?!*) But better than blissful ignorance (by a lot) is when I catch myself noticing the thought, "Those types of people can't drive," and pushing pause on the thought *as it computes* and reorienting my internal dialogue (with compassion, not harshness) to say, "No, Susan, that PERSON seemed to be swerving in the road and appeared to be driving in an unsafe way." My point: I am a fellow traveler; self-awareness is a practice.

We all have biases and stereotypes, and we will be confronted with the biases of others. I am inspired by Yolanda Conyers, who shares her own reflections on the role bias has played in her life.

HOW I DID IT

Lenovo's Yolanda Conyers On Beating Bias

"A hidden figure has to do more to overcome biases and stereotypes because people often make assumptions about them before they can prove and demonstrate their value," Yolanda explains. "In other words, they can't bring their whole selves into the workplace."

Yolanda leads HR strategies for Lenovo's Global Corporate functions and serves as chief diversity officer. She is responsible for retention and hiring strategies, as well as creating initiatives that align with business objectives to support leadership, promote talent development, and sustain a culture of inclusion. She is the corporate champion for increasing and leveraging Lenovo's unique diversity and highly inclusive culture to empower people to transform its global organizations.

As an engineer by training, Yolanda is passionate about STEM education for girls and women, recognizing that science, technology, engineering, and math careers offer higher salaries and advancement, as well as impact on economies. She coauthored *The Lenovo Way*, a bestselling business book available in English, Chinese, and Russian translations that recounts navigating life in a new culture in Beijing after Lenovo's acquisition of IBM's PC Division in 2006. It describes how the company blended the best of Eastern and Western business cultures by harnessing collaboration and diversity as core strengths.

With all these phenomenal achievements, what biases may have delayed Yolanda's strong career trajectory? In her own words:

"A *hidden figure* is someone who experiences a bias because of the color of their skin, gender, language, religion, or nationality, just to name a few. So, how does this manifest in the workplace?

- They're not included in key meetings or social gatherings where often key information is shared or exchanged;

- They are not included in decision making;

- Their input or expertise is not sought or considered;

- Their contributions are not embraced or recognized.

"I've felt like a hidden figure. Navigating in high-tech corporations as an African American female hasn't always been easy. I've worked for companies whose core values include respect for diversity and inclusion, which is very important to me. However, I encountered individuals who do not uphold these core values. So, I was faced with how to manage these situations. Early in my career, I applied for financial sponsorship from my company to enroll in an MBA program. I was qualified. My direct manager thought I was qualified and supported me. However, the next-level, decision-making executive denied my request. When I met with him to discuss my request that he denied, he couldn't explain the reason for denying my request. A few years later, executive management changed, and I applied again. I was approved. I never gave up. I learned that resilience and tenacity breaks through even the toughest of barriers. I also learned the importance of having supportive leadership and sponsors who recognize my potential.

"I have experienced that awkward feeling of being the only one of my kind in the room. I have been in situations where I spoke up in meetings and no one listened or another person would repeat the same comment and get acknowledged. I missed out on being invited to the table for key discussions, attending parties and social gatherings where decision makers were discussing pertinent information for work and building relationships that transfer into the workplace—these things matter . . . a lot. This led me to feeling isolated and created a reinforcing cycle that made me feel less likely to contribute.

"Today, I am a senior executive, and over the years, I pushed through many barriers in the workplace. I don't have to force my way into conversations; in fact, I am sought out for my opinions or perspectives. It feels great to be valued and to have a sense of belonging. This is what employees who are hidden figures long for. I work with executives to ensure a strong culture of inclusion, which enables our employees to bring their entire selves, ideas, experiences, and talents to Lenovo. It is good for the employees and it is good for Lenovo. It makes us more creative, innovative, and a stronger company.

"Throughout my experiences dealing with bias and proving your value professionally and personally, I've learned a few simple rules that help me overcome these challenges:

- Remember it's their issue . . . not yours. Don't let your star be diminished because of someone else's bias.

- Create and leverage your team who can support, counsel, and be your advocate.

- Create a teachable moment when you see or experience conscious or unconscious bias.

- Have support systems outside of the workplace— trusted family or friends who can lift you up, no matter what.

- And finally, don't give up. Find ways to turn being a victim to becoming a victor.

"To this day, I still struggle with asking for what I want, whether it's the next big job or projects beyond the scope of my current role. Even at the executive level, I waiver sometimes between expressing strong ambition and lacking the confidence that I can do it. I think many women know what I'm talking about: The voice in your head that says 'I really want this, but I'm not sure I can do it—it might be over my head—so I shouldn't ask.'

"I've learned through experience this mental cycle wastes time, and now I try to find the courage to remain confident and make the ask. Having a strong support network of friends, mentors, and family who prop you up during the lows and keep you humble during the highs helps keep me grounded, which makes me a better leader and person. I'm grateful for this unconditional support."

TOO YOUNG TO UNDERSTAND?

A former colleague, Abri Holden, a mindfulness manager and leadership coach, can attest to the power of self-awareness in not only recognizing someone else's bias, but also standing up to it. First, Abri needed to tune into her thoughts and feelings about how some of the comments she was in receipt of landed for her. Then, she needed to get curious about it, move into Compassionate Center, and from that place, make requests.

The bias Abri identifies is ageism, and it has a few tricky and bizarre nuances in the workplace because its manifestation may not seem harmful, as evidenced by Abri's example:

"I am a white female in my thirties. I've been told: 'You're too young to understand that.' 'It's before your time.' *or* 'Sweetie, you wouldn't understand that.' That type of language has the potential to exclude people from the conversation, whether intended or not. Another woman on my team at a previous job kept calling me 'sweetie' and 'honey.' I noticed I was often triggered by this language and had to come clean with myself. It took courage, but I spoke up and said, 'I need to be honest with you. That language is a pet peeve of mine. I know it's nothing you intended to do, but I want to share the impact of our exchange and make a request for the future.'"

For Abri, the comments about her age were micro inequities, small or subtle slights that demean or marginalize the recipient. The result of these comments for Abri was that they took her right out of the conversation. "It's still a challenge, but I have to trust my voice to say what feels not right and name it and make a request for myself and the other person."

Ultimately, biases can wear your best people down. I wonder how many more times Abri's participation and contributions would have been minimized by another woman's ageist language had she not spoken up.

One of the best things women can do to impact gender parity is to become aware of implicit biases we have about other women—and actively support one another.

Abri suggests, "When I see women overtly be unsupportive or dismissive of other women (including myself), I have found it usually comes from a place of scarcity mentality, limited seats at the table or at a certain place or level, and so if I put someone else down or take them out of the conversation or even do it subtly, it also creates more space for me at the table. I don't know if it is intentional, but I notice it. I've had conversations with different women around this topic. The scarcity mentality holds us back in growing and moving forward together."

Warning: You may be the one who unconsciously says something that is received by another as ageist. The first step in all of this business about bias is to identify your own.

PLEASE JOIN ME: IDENTIFY YOUR OWN UNCONSCIOUS BIAS

To better understand some of your own unconscious biases, take one of the Implicit Association Tests by Harvard's Project Implicit: https://implicit.harvard.edu. This is a fantastic way to begin to get conscious about what you might not yet be aware of.

I recently took the "Gender-Career Implicit Association Test." In some ways, how I scored both surprised me and *didn't*. Here's what I learned: I am in the majority of web-respondents to this test in scoring a moderately "automatic association" (therefore, implicit bias) of 'Male with Career' and 'Female with Family' (32 percent of responders).

I suppose it is better than being part of the 24 percent who scored with a strong automatic association of male with career and female with family, yet I was a bit miffed. Isn't my entire storyline about my formative influences wrapped up in a balance of loving men who represent both family and career? If being raised primarily by a single father doesn't make a grown woman identify "male with family" with some ease, what on earth does?

How did I internalize (albeit moderately) that men = career and women = family? I believe it is because of the pressure I feel on a daily basis to be a *great* mom to my two daughters. The bar I set for myself is *high* for kicking ass at home *and* at work.

My results underscore what so many working mothers and/or caregivers live every day: The feeling we just aren't enough anywhere we go. Taking this Implicit Association Test woke me up to a deeply held belief (and one that is apparently in spite of, or perhaps because of, my childhood experiences) that I need to be *aware of.* I share more about the level of distraction my Inner Critic causes when I am confronted with how imperfect a mother I am in Chapter 6. But first . . .

The question we ask on each hurdle in our Advancing Women in Leadership Assessment instrument is also the work we women need to *do* on each hurdle. For the internal hurdle of bias, the prompt is: [She] . . . *is open minded and unlimited in her thinking about her own capability and potential to achieve.* It makes me sad to think of the number of women I have met from almost every continent on the globe who believe their potential and capability to advance is limited, for a variety of reasons. Examples include: Felt bias (no one sees her as having high potential); lack of opportunity in the company (low attrition, thus limited openings); lack of sponsorship (no one in power advocating on her behalf); the need to move geographically in order to advance; the fact that she has children and thus, the assumption is she wouldn't want to advance; the fact that she has home responsibility so she requires flexibility and this is deemed as a leadership non-starter; the list goes on. The follow-up question then is this: What current stories or beliefs or biases do you have about yourself that no longer serve you? Let me share my own example.

Many of us possess biases about things we prefer. Many of our preferences are what we have been good at, been told we are good at, or been told are good things by those we respect or who raised us. I was encouraged and applauded for my ability to "get things done." My dad's motto—the words I hear every time I close my eyes and channel his abundant spirit into my consciousness—are, "GO. FOR. IT." My bold, hardworking, action-orientation made me, *me*. I wore this moniker with pride.

I was a leader, a doer. (The description was once synonymous for me and one of my unconscious biases; more on that when we look at Proving Your Value in Chapter 5.) Need something done? You can count on me. I unconsciously tied my worthiness (my value as a human being) to my ability to get 'er done. The problem with that? When I wasn't "doing" (or leading with a lot of my own effort) or *going for it*, I wasn't okay. I wasn't worthy. And that caused me to feel unsuccessful.

One of my own answers to the question, "What deeply held belief(s) do you have about yourself that no longer serve you?" was somewhere in the mix of "you can count on me," "I'll do it," "if I don't do it, it won't get done well" (control), and ultimately, "I need to take action to perform at a clip second to none or others won't see my value." This deeply held bias for action has played out for me in ways I never meant nor fully understood until recent years, and my ability to lead hinges on reframing this internal bias.

EXQUISITE CURIOSITY IS THE ANSWER

The self-aware leader is curious about perceptions others have of them. As the fellow Linkage Women in Leadership Institute cochair, Carla Harris, reminds us often: Perception *is* the copilot to reality, and as such, we need to be curious about how we "land" with others. Are we making the impact we intend? Are we checking with others to ensure our intention and impact are aligned?

When I worked for a spin-off of the Harvard Negotiation Project from 2002 to 2007, I became disciplined in this practice. This spin-off, in part, brought the work of Roger Fisher and others who followed into the world. Two seminal (and bestselling) books served as the core of the work we did with clients: *Getting to Yes* and *Difficult Conversations*. The authors of *Getting to Yes* and *Difficult Conversations* didn't call this "self-awareness," but I would argue that that's what it is. The authors, as their apt subtitles read, knew that if we wanted to *negotiate agreement without giving in* or *discuss what matters most*, we *had* to acknowledge our impact and take responsibility when it might not have been aligned with our intention.

So, I was schooled by the best of the best and deeply believed that my commitment to practice curiosity (seeking to understand others' perspectives), combined with owning my contribution and any unintended impact my actions might have on those around me, fueled much of my professional success. Essentially, I believed that if I worked hard, was smart, was kind to others, practiced curiosity, and separated intention from impact, nothing could stop me.

And then I tripped over the power of the Inner Critic and the power of bias.

Getting curious about our own bias is the place we must start. Gliding over all of the hurdles rests on our ability to get curious with ourselves, and in developing a practice where we hold our self in warm regard and with compassion while we do. Where I see all leaders (men and women alike) trip up (and where I do, too) is when we don't bring a more intentional process of thinking and curiousness to the conclusions we reach. When leaders derail, lead with implicit bias, or have unintended impacts are the moments when there is no space between stimulus and response or conclusion. The art of self-awareness requires taking space and pausing between stimulus and response—first by thoughtfully questioning the conclusions we reach and sometimes deploying this on a moment-to-moment basis.

In Iris Bohnet's groundbreaking book, *What Works: Gender Equality by Design*, which is loaded with research-based checks and balances on bias, the chapter "De-Biasing Minds Is Hard" emphasizes that sometimes "our better natures do not whisper in our ears." But if you look closely at Bohnet's data collected by companies, universities, and governments in Australia, India, Norway, the United Kingdom, the United States, Zambia, and other countries, you would be inspired by the speed with which we could all flip biases on their weary heads. She calls the solutions "evidence-based interventions" that could be instantly adopted.

Introducing another blueprint for where bias may surface in our brains, the bestselling book *Thinking, Fast and Slow*, by Nobel Memorial Prize in Economics Laureate Daniel Kahneman, is equally impactful. In it, Kahneman takes us on a tour of the mind and explains the two systems that drive the way we think. System 1 is fast, intuitive, and emotional; System 2 is slower, more deliberative, and more logical. To master the Inner Critic and to scale any of the hurdles, we must activate System 2.

I would just add to remember the Compassionate Center folding its arms around you the moment you realize your System 1 is in the driver's seat, and especially when, in System 2, your curiosity reveals the impact produced by your System 1.

LIKEABILITY ROBS CREDIBILITY?
A DOUBLE BIND

While I have always been fascinated by how people get along and the science of relationships, it wasn't until my mid-twenties when I realized I may not be as gifted in the people department as I thought I was. First came the advice from a senior executive (man) at one of my first jobs that I might want to work on my "vulnerability" (I had to look up the definition of the word). Then came the results from my first 360 (raters were men and women), where my raters scored me lower on emotional intelligence than I scored myself. Hmmm. . . .

It turns out, and this is something I struggle with to this day, the unintended impact of my take-charge style at times leaves others feeling cast aside. Working with this awareness, and while holding myself in warm regard, I make a concerted effort to moderate my intensity and engage others more thoughtfully. I needed to become aware of some of my own actions that no longer served me (often a result of an exuberant knee-jerk, go-go-go style), and make a moment-to-moment choice to slow it down a bit. Slowing down, or shifting to my System 2 level of conscious awareness, is still hard for me; some days are better than others. What helps me pause is remembering that the deeply held belief that I needed to move quickly to get things done is no longer serving my efficacy as a leader.

Here is what I am now convinced is also true: I have faced a trade-off between being seen by others as competent *or* likeable over and over in my lifetime. I just didn't know it until I learned about the now well-documented Harvard Business School study, which is widely being used to demonstrate bias. As described by Lesley Symons and Herminia Ibarra in their illuminating April 2014 report, "What the Scarcity of Women in Business Case Studies Really Looks Like," for *Harvard Business Review*, different groups of students read a case study about a venture capitalist with one single difference—gender. Everything about the case study and the person is the same; however, in one case study, the name used is "Heidi" and the other, "Howard." Time and again in applications of this exercise, students respected both "Howard" and "Heidi," yet Howard was described as likeable and Heidi was seen as selfish and not "the type of person you would want to hire or work for." This phenomenon has become known as the "likeability penalty" or the "likeability bias." It goes like this: Success and likeability are positively correlated for men and negatively correlated for women. When a man is successful, his peers often like him more. When a woman is successful, both men and women often like her less. This trade-off between success and likeability creates a double bind for women. If a woman is competent, she does not seem nice enough, but if a woman seems really nice, she is considered less competent.

Until about two years ago, I never knew that the cost of being liked was having my competence questioned. Or, that the cost of my successes/competence might leave me as seen as less likeable. Have you experienced this weird phenomenon in which you are questioned about possessing both competence and likeability? If you're unsure, it kind of feels surreal—receiving a suspicious reaction to being naturally personable and intelligent, as if both traits cannot coexist in a human being.

Let me set the record straight here, as I do now in every talk I give: I am both competent and likeable. My bet is that you are, too. You are smart. You, like me, have grown businesses and product lines or brought ideas to high-impact action. You have marshalled the resources of others to manifest a vision that has and continues to impact others. Being likeable didn't hurt in these successes, but let's be clear: You are *as competent* as you are likeable.

I have images of a not-too-much younger version of myself, enthusiastically (even gleefully) running fast around a track only to stumble. But whatever hurdle that was there was, in fact, invisible. I stood up, brushed myself off, and set out again.

For a girl who doesn't run hurdles, I've done a lot of running . . . and falling.

I can only presume that this likeability bias has negatively impacted my career. I believed in meritocracy until I was passed up a time or three in subtle and not so subtle ways—not just for jobs, but for my opinion about things. I walked away from meetings and discussions feeling tolerated, even listened to, but not heard. I have been confused about why, when I have had ample successes, leaders at different phases of my life in different organizations didn't see me as someone competent enough to lead more than what I had been leading.

Apparently, what is seen (and, arguably, celebrated) as entrepreneurship, self-confidence, and vision in a man is perceived as arrogance and self-promotion in a woman. This explains so much of what I have sensed about my impact (but no matter how much self-awareness I had, wasn't changing). Take the growth of Linkage's Women in Leadership Institute as an example. While I credit the success and impact the Institute has enjoyed to many men and women who have served to lead and support it (colleagues, faculty, participants, etc.) I have and continue to put myself "out there" as a brand ambassador of the event. Emceeing for a few years, then joining the ranks of keynote faculty, and eventually serving as cochair, was a strategic choice on my part based on the hypothesis that the event would grow if there was explicit and formal affiliation with a person—a courageous woman leader. This took courage, involved a vision, and a good dose of self-confidence to pull off. It was nerve wracking to act out my Inner Critic on stage—and I kept reminding myself that I'm doing it for the purpose of helping other women come to compassion. Yet over the years, I have heard whispers that some have perceived that I involved myself purely out of self-interest and self-promotion. To this day, thinking of these critiques and judgements can make me angry. I have come to believe that there is a limit to what I can do to change this perception, or bias, of my role with the success of the Institute. What I *can* do is inspire and involve others to engage with me to ensure the Institute continues to have impact. Today, the very capable, smart, and professional Kerry Seitz serves as the Executive Director. Today, the event is her ship; she is the captain. I serve on her faculty, and as an advisor and cochair.

Coaching and supporting her (and many of the capable women who came before her) in her leadership of our nearly 20-year old flagship, Linkage's Women in Leadership Institute, helps me to cast aside the accusation that I am only in this for myself. At some level, we need to trust our own true agenda over the way a common bias may make it appear to others.

The term *double bind* was first used in the 1950s by the anthropologist Gregory Bateson to describe situations in communication when an individual (or group) receives two or more conflicting messages, and one message negates the other. My double bind was and still is leading (even more slowly and more thoughtfully) at the risk of being seen by some as less competent and by others as less likeable. What do I do about it? I have come to terms with the fact that not everyone is going to like me. I'd rather make game-changing impact and work with people who believe in my good intentions, than sit around and stew about who doesn't like me. This is a moment-to-moment practice of self-compassion that keeps it all okay.

This double bind may be the fuel to your clarity, the next hurdle we take on.

CHAPTER 4

CLARIFY WHAT YOU'RE UP FOR

Hurdle: Clarity

The Big Question

Do I know what I want? How can I create a promising future in which I am intentional about my professional advancement?

The Big Lie

It isn't important to take time to think about what I want for myself and plan accordingly.

The Big Opportunity

Purposefully keeping an eye on achieving what I really want for myself.

The Inner Critic at Work on Clarity

One-up: "If I didn't need to overcompensate for others, I'd have time to be more strategic about my career."

One-down: "I'm not qualified for what I really want, and no one would support it anyway."

What You Must Change to Run Over This Hurdle

- Listen to the whispers of your heart, focus on where your unique gifts and talents are in service of others, and discover your calling and the power of purpose.

- Create ways to ensure your work allows for this part of you to show up.

- Make time for reflection and discussion.

WHAT ARE WE TALKING ABOUT *REALLY*?

When this hurdle first came into focus, I initially referred to it as "ambivalence." From female doctors working in academic medicine, to women in various functional jobs in financial services, to women working for technology and automotive and consumer packaged goods companies, I observed a clear hurdle rearing its ugly head: When the topic of "what do I want next for myself professionally" came up, women expressed a good bit of ambiguity, or even ambivalence. At first, and because I was asking for women to raise their hands in a group setting if they knew what they wanted their next professional step to be, I thought perhaps so few raised their hands for fear of being called on.

So, we switched our approach, asking for confidential written polls in our webinars and other work. The same result presented itself: The vast majority (95% +/-) of women who we asked if they knew what they wanted next simply said: "not really" or just "No—I don't have any clue."

This phenomenon made me pause. Could this be why women aren't advancing into positions of leadership? Is it because we're unsure or unclear about what it is we want for ourselves, and thus, we aren't advocating for ourselves? Worse yet, are we promoted into jobs we don't want and decide to leave? Will we get the advocacy of others if we remain uncertain about our aim?

I think this *is* part of why some women aren't advancing, but sadly, it alone doesn't come near to answering why those who get clear or who have always been clear about what it is they strive for aren't stepping into leadership at the same clip as men. The answer for why women who *do* have clarity about what they want, but who aren't seeing the progress they want in their career, can be answered, in part, in the chapters ahead.

Linkage Global Institute for Leadership Development® faculty member, Rhodes scholar, and author of *The Coaching Habit: Say Less, Ask More & Change the Way You Lead Forever*, Michael Bungay Stanier, refers to the question of "what do you want" as "the Goldfish Question," noting that this question "often elicits slightly bugged eyes, and a mouth opening and closing with no sound coming out." While a hilarious description, it's in sync with my findings, too.

In my experience, if you are clear about what you want, yet you aren't advancing, you may be:

- Doing too much, and thus proving your value in the job you have—unintentionally refraining from letting go, equipping, inspiring, and enabling others. (This is the hurdle of adding too much value, to be addressed in Chapter 5.)

- Implicitly or explicitly believing that you are not deserving, ready, or capable of the next step. (This is the hurdle of recognized confidence, to be addressed in Chapter 6.)

- Believing your brand and presence speaks for itself or has impact that may be different than your desired intentions. (This is the hurdle of brand and presence, to be addressed in Chapter 7.)

- Thinking that the right people know what you want when they don't. (This is the hurdle of asking for what you want, to be addressed in Chapter 8.)

- Assuming that building and leveraging relationships among those who are in positions of power is not as important as that all-consuming to-do list, and consequently, pushing networking aside as a nice-to-have; therefore, you may not be on the radar of those who make talent decisions. (This is the hurdle of networking, to be addressed in Chapter 9.)

- Or, lastly, you may be facing more than your fair share of bias from those who have the ability to create the movement you want for yourself, or you may not have the sponsorship needed to manifest what you want professionally. (I addressed the hurdle of Bias in Chapter 3.)

Yet, as I work with and learn from women from all over the world who have participated in experiences taken from Linkage's *Advancing Women Leaders* educational experiences, I find that clarity is a journey, and "checking in" with yourself on a regular basis really matters. Tapping into the same muscle (conscious awareness) used to notice your thoughts and feelings, you must ask yourself, "What do I want for myself?"

Interestingly, when it comes to desire, women are much more inclined to ask what others want and adjust their schedules, assets, and strategies to meet those needs on an epic scale. Are you one of the guilty ones?

In his piece for *Forbes*, "4 Skills that Give Women a Sustainable Advantage Over Men," contributor Glenn Llopis describes one of these skills: "Women are natural givers: . . . Women enjoy living their lives through a cause that serves the advancement and acceleration of societal needs. This is why in the workplace women are great at inspiring and lifting those around them. This is why most women leaders are such excellent long-term strategic thinkers."

Sarah Bettman, a diversity expert and leader, advocates that there can be a cost to all this giving if you don't have a strong foundation of clarity to help set the boundaries. "I like to joke that I took an accidental detour out of college from being on a management consultant path and ended up as a firefighter paramedic. After 10 years in emergency services it became clear that the hurdle I needed to scale was also the biggest life changer and that was clarity. I didn't know what I wanted for my life in high school and college. I retrospectively understand now that I based what I wanted on what I thought others needed or expected from me. Because I tend to be a driven person, I accomplished many of the things I set out to do, but without clarity around the things I truly wanted, I did a lot of things that never quite fulfilled me. When I was in emergency service, I found the job to be compelling and the community to be my family, but it was not what I wanted to do with my life. I remember thinking, 'I save lives for a living, but it's not enough, and then wondered what was wrong with me. I was a high performer, I had sponsors, I had a future in that career, but after I retired, I found I needed to figure out what I was about first. Ten years later, I am happy to say I have figured it out, but it was work. I have since learned that I want to be of service and to help people live better lives. I was doing that in emergency services, but it was the right idea in the wrong place. When asked about clarity, many think about the role they want, but it is not about role; it's about the activities. It's essential to think about the activities you like doing, what you're good at and want to do more of. If you share that you want to do those activities, it makes it easier for others to help you do more of that. For example, prior to my most recent career move I shared with others that I wanted to build something. I didn't know the title, but I knew the work. I was able to use that information as I considered new roles and then as I negotiated for my current role. Now I am building a diversity and inclusion program within a large organization. I finally feel like I am the person I always wanted to be. It just took clarity to get there."

Linkage defines clarity as knowing who you are and what you want as you advance. It rests on knowing the value you bring. As leaders advance and engage in new assignments and responsibilities, their sense of themselves as leaders expands and grows. We assess in our Women in Leadership Assessment for "clarity" as follows: "Projects a compelling future vision for who she wants to be as a leader and/or how she wants to contribute in the working world."

HOW I DID IT

LPL Financial's Melissa Master-Holder On Unearthing Clarity

Melissa's background is in organizational effectiveness and performance consulting. An expert in leadership development, she works from the space of design thinking (human-centered design thinking) and innovation, helping users do better and be better. Melissa has worked in a variety of organizations and industries including running the coaching division and content development group for life coach and bestselling author Tony Robbins' Anthony Robbins Companies.

Melissa has had a great deal of diverse opportunities and successes. Along the way, she has confronted—and mastered—the hurdle of clarity and now coaches others on how they can, too. Here, she explains.

"Over the years, I have lacked clarity of what I wanted to be, how I wanted to show up, what I felt like I could do. I lacked clarity on how I could contribute and what I was deserving of. I am a mom of four (three adult daughters and one teen son). Every time I say I have four kids, people drop their jaw. How can you be a good mom? I've had a lot of that. The stereotype is that a mom can't be good in both places (home and work), and you can't have it all. I've always been very career-driven and never thought I would not be a career-oriented person. When I was young and started in my career of banking, I didn't have a perception I was different, that as a woman, I would not be executive VP. I was raised in a home where my parents were very liberal, giving, with a high expectation of owning who you are and having confidence. Early in my career, I was told in a meeting that I was 'too young' to share my perspective and that as a woman I needed to recognize I didn't yet understand where my life was going, that I was not married and 'needed' to have children. It was the first time I thought, *Maybe I can't do what I want to do*.

"I went to my dad and said, 'Maybe I'm not supposed to be doing all this.' He said, 'Take 50 percent of what that person said and then look up and figure out what is next for yourself.' I got married, got my business degree, had children. I was constantly looking for how I could grow and contribute. It wasn't until my fourth child that I faced this stereotype again. I was working in the restaurant business at the time and when I told the CEO, 'I am pregnant, I am going out on leave,' he looked at me and said, 'Wow, why would you do that?' He continued, 'You already have three. You will never advance your career. Are you ever coming back to work?'

"I had four kids, got my degree, advanced my career—it was never easy, but it was my choice. I had wanted all of these things. I ended up leaving that company because I had the clarity that my effort was worthy of a different mindset from management.

"Each of us has our own story and own choices and that is why the hurdles are different for each of us. I recognize that the choices I make and decisions I have will present different hurdles because of what I am living. I had to own that first. I have learned not to give permission to other people to make my hurdles harder. I own them and manage them. I surround myself with situations and people that help me manage—not amplify—differing hurdles when they present themselves. When I'm in situations that heighten them, I work with the voices in my head (my Inner Critic among them) and ask myself what is most important for me in this situation? I coach others to take this approach as well. Clarity comes from checking in with ourselves, with getting clear about what it is that we need and want. It is about belonging to yourself first, giving to others, and living your true 'all.'"

CLARITY AND SERVICE

Clarity is freedom from ambiguity, which may come from not knowing your priorities or not identifying your values. For some, these values include love, health, family, community, and making a difference in the world. For others, achievement, wealth, creativity, and success are high on the list. For the sake of this book, let's assume most people who have identified their top values uphold a combination of these. The reason that priorities and values intersect here is that they tend to drive most of our decisions. If you are secure in your decision and the outcome is undesirable, the disappointment isn't nearly as intense because you always gain further clarity and continue to walk through open doors. You are resting strongly in your priorities and values. However, when you lack clarity, you're tremendously vulnerable. This is the vulnerability that comes from being in the big, bad world of whatever area you are stewing in uncertainty around.

You're on the road to clarity though, as soon as you are self-aware that you have to get clear.

As with all of the hurdles, I have tripped over clarity repeatedly and in a fairly meaningful way. I found myself in my mid-thirties with two kids under the age of five, engaged in the same kind of work I had been doing for most of my working life: helping to market, sell, and grow someone else's idea, brand, thought leadership, book, concept, and/or business. I love representing ideas that make a difference. I love working with others to galvanize revenue-producing participation. I have had the good fortune of working for organizations that bring game-changing experiences to individuals and organizations so they can better their relationships, their goals, their leadership, their impact, their lives, and the lives of those they love and/or serve. The people with whom I have worked have been the best in their business. I have had roles in business management, strategic marketing, business development, and product and solution development. My favorites were when I was able to create something that had not yet been created—or build on something that existed, and engage others in manifesting the vision. Yet, at thirty-five, I found it hard to tune out what was a nagging (albeit, whispering) voice inside my head saying: "What about your voice, your learning, your ability to teach?" Usually, when I heard this "inner whisper," my Inner Critic was at the ready to shoot it down with a swift, "Seriously, Susan, you don't have your PhD, you didn't go to an Ivy League school, you aren't teaching at an academic institution; you are the one who builds the business, but you can't be the one who has the idea that sells."

As if that weren't enough, I was told a few times in a variety of ways that this critical voice was accurate. I was told that I was good at my job (which was awesome because it was affirming that I was effective), yet I wanted to do more than what I was being affirmed for (namely, marketing and selling). One former thought leader with whom I worked actually said: "Susan Brady, you'll always be second banana. You're not the one who people want to hear from. I am." I have heard from other women that they, too, have been encouraged to keep their heads down and continue to perform at what they are tasked with. This is discouraging, as it gives us permission—even encourages us—to squelch the whispers of our heart. It is also why some women can't or won't articulate what they want next for themselves. It can feel too risky to admit that there might be more you can do than what you are working on currently.

Hearing that I wasn't the one others wanted to hear from was an early indication that working for thought leaders/authors/experts was a sure way of keeping my inferiority complex intact. It was becoming clear that my Inner Critic was loving her new job: to dash any hope of having a unique voice or contribution to the field of leadership and relationship management other than learning and selling the greats.

I couldn't shake it. I had been a business partner to some of the best teachers in my field. The synthesis of my learning from all of these people had to count for something! Even when a close friend asked me, "What would you say if you were at a podium, looking at 500 people?" I didn't have the answer. I had never thought about that before, but the question intrigued (and tortured) me. To find the answer, I read lots of books, talked to lots of people, and decided to take on the discovery of the answer as if it were my job. Things didn't begin to get clear for me until I realized one thing. My clarity came when I set out to use my gifts and talents in service of others.

Pay attention to that whispering voice
telling you what you want.

I believe that, at some level, we know what we want for ourselves. We know what our unique gifts are. If you are saying to yourself, *Really, Susan? Because I don't*, stay with me. Often, the clues about what we want are all around us. We just haven't listened or seen them or allowed ourself to believe them. A great place to start is to think about what it is you have done in the working world that has made you joyful. What are the two or three times in your career when you were fully engaged and feeling like you were bringing your unique value?

Fast-forward to 2014, when the president and CEO of Linkage Asia, Sam Lam, encouraged me to serve as one of Linkage's keynotes at Linkage's Women in Leadership Institute. I gave Sam a million reasons why this was a bad idea. He was adamant and got others to encourage me, too. And I was terrified. I wasn't terrified to get on stage. That part came naturally for me after years of acting in theatre and emceeing work events. I was terrified to be on stage *to share my own thinking, to deliver lines that I wrote*. I know what makes for a great speaker—usually a blend of a helpful model or framework combined with great storytelling. What was it that I was uniquely qualified to talk about, *that would be in service of 600+ women and their advancement?* My Inner Critic was having a field day.

This last question around being of service to the participants ruled out a number of no-brainer talks, including: how to feed kids and never use anything but the microwave, how to work with high-ego individuals, how to do too much . . .

Around the same time, I facilitated a Linkage public virtual webinar on the things women leaders must deal with—one being their Inner Critic. The webinar itself had an astonishing 800+ registrations, and in one of the webinar polls, we asked what trips you up the most. The majority (over 80 percent of respondents) voted for their Inner Critic. This gave me an idea: What if I act out my Inner Critic and show women leaders how to get back to a place of Compassionate Center? I could tell stories of moments when I second-guessed, bashed, put-down, judged, was merciless, and generally contempt-filled for myself. I could also admit to moments when I thought others *just didn't get it* and how good and natural my own self-righteous indignation feels. We could laugh! And learn! I could use myself as an instrument for what MUST be a dialogue in the minds of more than just a few. The opportunity for all could be the notion that if I can master my Inner Critic, anyone can. I would teach them what I have learned along the way from the best relationship and leadership thinkers in our lifetime about self-awareness. (Let's not confuse this newfound clarity about how I could use my unique gifts to help others with the level at which I was dreading being vulnerable in front of hundreds of people.)

I decided to do what bestselling author and nationally-acclaimed shame, vulnerability, and courage researcher, Brené Brown, calls "dare greatly," and I stepped on stage at Linkage's Women in Leadership Institute and delivered my very first keynote address ever to a ballroom of 650 incredibly impressive women in business. What I didn't know was that, over the course of the coming years, the stories women would tell me about their Inner Critic voices would lead to *clarity* about common themes where they struggle most, and ultimately, result in the seven hurdles in this book.

PURPOSE AND CALLING MATTERS

Richard Leider can best be described as the "father of the purpose movement." Richard is a purpose guru and the author of

10 books, including three bestsellers, and his work has been translated into 21 languages. *Repacking Your Bags* and *The Power of Purpose* are considered classics in the personal growth field. He also serves as the cochair of Linkage's Global Institute for Leadership Development, a deeply immersive leadership journey built on Linkage's Purposeful Leadership™ model.

Full disclosure: It is Richard's work on calling and purpose that helped me on my journey of clarity the most. And it is Richard's work that I return to in moments where I have a decision to make about what's next for me.

Richard was kind enough to chat with me about the hurdle of clarity, answering four questions that I believe will help you the most with the hurdle of clarity.

Q: *Why is it important to know our purpose?*

A: "Knowing our purpose is essential; it is not a luxury or only for the affluent or the wealthy. It is, in fact, fundamental to our health, our healing, our longevity, our productivity, and our prosperity."

Q: *What's the difference between a calling and a purpose?*

A: "Everyone has unique gifts (talents). A calling is the vocational expression of purpose; your calling is your gifts at work in your life. Your calling is how you are bringing your purpose into work every day. Your calling is your contribution. Being clear about your calling gives you a reason to get up in the morning beyond yourself and it connects with your work. Given that we spend 60 percent or more of our lives in the workplace, we want to be sure we are contributing using our gifts."

Q: *How can we efficiently find out what it is that we want for ourselves professionally?*

A: "I have two 'efficient' ways anyone can get clear about their purpose. I call the first quick way the 'Gotta Minute School of Coaching.' Here's the formula: Gifts + Passion + Values = Purpose. Write down your 1) *Gifts* (talents you are born with or acquired that are still with you), add your 2) *Passions* (your interests) + *Values* (where you love to use your gifts; where you have voice in matters), and this equals your *Purpose at Work*.

"The second quick way to get clear about your purpose is universal and something I call the Mirror Test: Take out a yellow Post-it note. Write the words 'grow and give' on it and stick it on your bathroom mirror. When you wake up, ask yourself: 'How am I going to grow and give today?' At the end of the day before you go to bed, ask yourself, 'How did I grow and give today?'"

Q: *What are your favorite questions to get folks to the answers they are seeking?*

A: "I researched elders—people 65 years old and older—and asked them, if they could live life over again, what they would do differently. Three themes emerged from the research: they would be more reflective, they would be more courageous, and they would be more purposeful. The questions that I believe are most helpful include: What is success to you? What is the good life? What are your practices? Why do you get up in the morning?"

One of the tools in Richard's vast arsenal is a deck of fifty-two cards he calls "Calling Cards™." These cards can help users discover an increased awareness about their unique gifts. As a result of working with the cards, I became clear that my calling (and thus, what I ultimately need to be able to give in any job I have) includes: Awakening Spirit, Getting Participation, Getting to the Heart of Matters, Making Connections, and Advancing Ideas. This book is a direct action of this clarity and synthesis of ideas that hopefully crystalize for you.

Part of getting clear about what you want is accepting your gifts and talents and loving yourself. (More on this in Chapter 6, Recognized Confidence.)

HIDDEN OPPORTUNITIES FOR CLARITY

Cynthia Tragge-Lakra is the chief talent and transformation officer for Synchrony Financial, a consumer finance business with 16,000 global employees. You may see terms like talent and transformation in her "chief" title and assume that her road to clarity was a short one. It was not. Because her mother was an entrepreneur who started a family business in telephone and telecommunications, Cynthia grew up thinking everyone just played roles that were needed to get the job done. Everybody did everything. Some people were better at one thing than another, but everyone just figured it out.

"Especially when you're young and trying to fit in and you don't know what you don't know, it is hard to distinguish learning to be a good leader versus learning to fit in in a strong culture," explains Cynthia. "I didn't always distinguish the two. Even when you ask for what you want, the answers are not as clear, so you go along for the ride of people tapping you on the shoulder with, 'We'd like for you to do this, we'd like for you to do that.' Before you know it, you're in a spot where you're not really sure how you ended up there. That is probably my weakness on clarity. I've always had clarity for everything except my career. Even if I would ask for what I wanted, I wouldn't stick with it. In corporate cultures, I think it is seductive because there is so much infrastructure and support around you, it 'appears' you're learning a lot.

"If I were to give advice to younger people: every couple of years, you should do something completely different. Change companies. I don't think anyone should stay more than 10 years max. You can always reinvent yourself cross-functionally, but the organizational culture slows down your learning in any company because you start to lose that external perspective. Adapting to new environments keeps you on your toes. It refreshes you. It reminds you of skills you probably had that you weren't using somewhere else, and it makes you work harder. Moving between environments will continue to challenge you. That truly builds leadership skills. In my role today—with clarity—I tell employees to make themselves uncomfortable and to always have something outside of work that keeps them engaged and interested. That balances out the Inner Critic a little bit. It's not as loud if you have a full life professionally and personally."

CREATING THE CONDITIONS
FOR GETTING CLEAR

Dr. Tara Swart is a neuroscientist, leadership coach, award-winning author, and medical doctor, as well as a Linkage Women in Leadership Institute faculty member. In her research about what conditions our brain requires to become clear, she's found that each and every one of us can take specific actions that will set us up to be in peak condition so that we are able to have clarity about our purpose and lives.

Criticality of Sleep

Dr. Swart explained that job #1 is getting enough sleep. "If you're tired, your brain won't let you do any higher thinking; it will just help you survive. We need to rest our brain, so that we can do the hard work of 'what do I really want.' Tara recommends 7–9 hours of sleep per night. She was quick to point out that only 1–2 percent of the population can operate on full brain capacity with less than 7–9 hours a night. Further, the power to override the Inner Critic is only available to us if our brain has had rest. For restful sleep, she wants us to slumber in a dark, quiet room, where we have no interruptions.

Criticality of Diet

While Dr. Swart is quick to point out that there are lots of healthy diets for boosting our brains, for a busy woman, snacking small and often (up to six times daily) is essential to making clear, purposeful decisions. She explained, "The average brain weighs 4–5 lbs, but it uses 25–30 percent of the breakdown products of what you eat. When there is no supply, you literally go into scarcity thinking. You can't think long term, you can't think strategically; 1–3 percent dehydrated means your neurons can't communicate and can't make the best decisions." She shared that she always eats something before a coaching session or client meeting, because the brain research is clear and she understands that her mental performance is going to be much better if she is fueled. Dr. Swart suggests eating smaller amounts more regularly and drinking plenty of water. "By the time you know you're thirsty, you are way more than 3 percent dehydrated." (This comment made me notice that I was, in fact, thirsty and that I had not yet had a full glass of water, nearly 5 hours into my day. Cue the water bottle fill. Inner Critic, sit down. I'm learning, too.)

Criticality of Oxygen and Movement

When Dr. Swart said, "Oxygen is very important," I couldn't help but chuckle. I quickly learned she meant business: "Stressed people 'breath hold'—taking very shallow breaths. Having a practice of breathing deeply allows your brain to work at full capacity." Further, we need to move our bodies! "Taking at least 10,000 steps a day and doing 150 minutes of aerobic exercise a week will resource your brain for higher thinking."

Criticality of Mindfulness

Dr. Swart insisted that, "Any mindfulness activity like yoga or meditation that connects your mind and body has been shown to reduce stress hormones like cortisol. In fact, we now know that women who do yoga three times a week have less stress (lower levels of cortisol) than women of the same age who don't." Note to self: do more yoga.

Let's review Dr. Swart's brilliant, and very actionable, advice so far about all the things, ideally, we need to do to put our mental resources into high gear: keeping sleep hours high, hydration levels high, glucose (not refined sugars) levels consistent, oxygen levels high, and cortisol levels low. WE CAN DO THIS!

CHOICE REDUCTION

Sadly, we can't do everything all the time, and if you do feel strongly about showing up for others, it's important you pace yourself and realize you have limited hours in the day. Dr. Swart's remedy for the depletion of brain power that occurs when we're doing too much and/or are stressed, is something she calls "choice reduction." (You will see in Chapter 5 on Proving Your Value, I am a self-professed do-too-mucher—you probably know the feeling.) On this, her advice is to, "Understand you have a limited amount of resources for thinking each day." Let's repeat that statement with the most important word emphasized: "You have a limited amount of resources for *thinking* each day." Like others, you probably get tired and stressed sometimes. I do. I believe that my time is my most precious (diminishing) resource, but often think my energy, including mental, is plentiful. It never occurred to me that I had a limited amount of resources for *thinking*. Dr. Swart recommends a strict morning routine and making relatively minor decisions the night before (what to wear tomorrow, what to have for breakfast, if you have children, planning out the same for them, etc.). "This simple planning leaves you with the brain space to focus elsewhere." Planning ahead for the often mundane things we do each day and having a routine means we get to spend more brain energy on things that bring us joy and make us feel *on purpose*!

Owning Past Success

Dr. Swart strongly suggests keeping a list of compliments you get or achievements you make. I have suggested this to my coaching clients often and call this a "personal value document" (as in "how you add value"). More on this tool in Chapter 6 on Recognized Confidence. But her rationale was (of course) linked to proven brain research, which shows that, when we are confronted with doing something new or taking a risk, going back to a list of compliments or achievements can boost our brain's believability that we can accomplish what's before us. She suggests, "Ask yourself: 'Have I ever done anything like that?'" Look for what might be in common with what you are seeking to do and your list. Further (and I *loved* this) she suggests, "If you haven't done that specific thing, you can borrow from other's successes. There will come a time when you're trying to achieve something you haven't done before. If your brain thinks that something is impossible, you're less likely to achieve it. If there is no evidence that something is achieved, your brain won't allow you to believe it. Change how your brain operates."

Digital Detox

Aren't female brains better at multitasking than male brains? Can't we do more at the same time? To this myth, the doctor says, "NOT TRUE." Every time we multitask, we do each task less well. Taking what she calls a "digital detox" is one way to create more mental space. "If you have the privilege of taking time off to think about your purpose (and I mean longer than an hour or a day—more like a week), make it a digital-free time. You can do mind wandering if you turn something off. Take some time to step back. Getting clear about what you want for yourself requires the ability to let the mind wander, and mind wandering requires a digital free environment."

CREATING CLARITY

You've been reading about clarity and learning exclusive keys to it, like identifying your values, owning past successes, detoxing from devices, and determining how a lack of clarity may have prohibited you from advancing in your career or life as a whole. Now it's time to conquer this hurdle!

1. Get in the right frame of mind.

In addition to the very helpful advice provided by Dr. Tara Swart above, here are a few simple activities that have helped me and those I coach to help you discover how your own gifts and talents can best be used in service of others—at work. Like many, you may find yourself at times spending more time doing things that zap your energy and/or don't fuel you. It is usually on these ever-so-exhausting days that you may be confronted with the question: "What do I want?" This is when you know you need to schedule time to reflect on the answer.

Chances are you will be naturally motivated to "get clear" about what you want when you can't stand the inner (or outer) level of complaint you hear yourself engaging in about your current reality. Perhaps you'll be more intrinsically motivated to take on clarity if you don't feel satisfied with your current state. My hope is that you can be more proactive. There doesn't need to be anything wrong with your current situation in order to take time to think about what it is that you want.

If you need a five-minute fix on any given day to take yourself from a Negative Nelly place to one where you feel personally inspired and empowered, find Carla Harris. (This may be when you notice that your Inner Critic is going OFF on someone or something that annoys you. When you push pause and begin to get curious, you can then ask yourself, "Okay, if not this, then what?") I especially like and recommend, "Carla Harris Gives Career Advice to Her 25-Year Old Self," a video she did for women in her home workplace of Morgan Stanley.

Oh, and if you need to journal and get off your chest all in your current state that annoys you, have at it. Get out the ugly so you can turn to the good stuff. If you aren't "seeking" clarity already, I encourage you to do so. At the heart of your life and your leadership is *you*. Take the time to think about your future.

2. Make time for reflection.

As with anything we want to manifest, getting clear about what we want requires our intention about how and when we devote our time to it. I am an early riser (I get up with the sun on most days) and this peaceful, quiet time in my home is when I have done my best reflection about what I want. Sometimes I need to officially schedule time in my calendar for me to think, write, reflect, or do one of the many vision exercises we at Linkage invite our coaching clients to explore.

One of the most helpful assignments I received from my former coach, Joanne Brem, who I feature in Chapter 6 on Recognized Confidence, was to get some colored pencils and a blank piece of paper and draw pictures of what I wanted in my life. That was her only direction. Though not "pretty," this exercise was very insightful. Try this on your own journey: Write words and circle them. Draw pictures of things you want to do more of. Have fun with the colors. You may be surprised by what you put on the page. When I was done with this exercise, I tilted my head to one side and thought to myself, *Wow, for someone who says she isn't clear about what it is that she wants, you sure did fill this page!*

3. Ask for help.

It can be from your best friend, from a trusted colleague (or a few), or from a professional coach. Frankly, asking for help for the purpose of gaining clarity about what you want is a great way to practice *asking*—something you'll need to do when you figure out what it is that you want. Asking (when it benefits you, specifically) is a hurdle that emerged from our work, and so I devote an entire chapter to it in Chapter 8.

What were you doing the last time you felt joyful at work (engaged and happy and feeling like you were making a difference all at the same time)? Be specific. Where were you? Who were you surrounded by? What specifically were you doing? If this is hard for you to answer, you may be doing too much. The racing around to get it all done may be preventing you from seeing the moments that bring you fulfillment with clarity.

And this is why we need to address the hurdle of Proving Your Value.

CHAPTER 5

MOVE BEYOND SELF-RELIANCE: EQUIP AND EMPOWER OTHERS

Hurdle: Proving Your Value

The Big Question

How do I stop doing too much?

The Big Lie

Working to the point of exhaustion and proving my value by doing too much will eventually pay off with great accolades and financial rewards and promotions galore.

The Big Opportunity

Shift doing it all to influencing, inspiring, equipping and enabling others (your future followers), and enjoying your life more.

The Inner Critic at Work on Proving Your Value

One-up: "If other people could do things as well as I do them, I wouldn't need to do so much."
One-down: "I am not adding value."

What You Must Change to Run Over This Hurdle

- Don't let perfection be the enemy of *good enough*.

- Be selective about what you do (requires *clarity*)— say *no*!

- Equip yourself to inspire and influence others. Focus on letting go of control, asking for help, and coaching and encouraging others.

- Recognize the difference between healthy striving and an addiction to busyness.

WHAT ARE WE TALKING
ABOUT *REALLY*?

As I speak to and work with individual women, groups of women leaders, and those around them, what I hear most often is how busy we women are. I have yet to come across a woman who is driven to achieve and not feeling a tad (or extremely) overwhelmed about the volume of things she is managing in her life. They include, but are not limited to: planning, leading, and recapping meetings; business-as-usual duties and net-new initiatives toward the big corp. picture; updating social media (which sometimes leads to more contacts, more commitments); working out or at least engaging in some level of movement with their bodies because they've been at a desk or dinner table all day, all night; and all the tasks involved in being a great (rather than just breathing) boss, partner, mother, family member, friend, and/or pet caretaker. Anything I missed? Maybe fun? Sun?

This hurdle is, at the core, about how and on what we are spending our time. This hurdle is about asking ourselves daily if what we are doing and if the volume of energy we are expending is truly in our best service and the best service of those around us. Research led by University of California, Berkeley and INSEAD professor, Morten T. Hansen, reveals that doing less (or "mastering selectivity" as he calls it) is essentially the ticket to getting ahead. He wrote about this phenomenon in his latest book, *Great at Work: How Top Performers Do Less, Work Better, and Achieve More.*

The analogy I use when speaking about this hurdle is rowing a boat. Picture this: You, awesome woman, are alone in your (smallish) boat. You have oars to row with to keep you going. The exuberance of rowing your own boat may have started in your formative years, like in high school. You manage your academics, your extra-curricular activities, your friends, and your family. You are rewarded for this elegant and powerful rowing, and graduate to college where you fine-tune the art of rowing your boat. In these early years of life, you even pull the boat over once in a while, get out, stretch, and play between long "shifts" of rowing. Or maybe you have friends who are rowing their own boats alongside you, and the feeling of being together and having a unified group and purpose (be that to study for a test or lead a campus effort) is exhilarating. You have evidence of the fruit of your labor and effort since you get *more* opportunities!

As your life becomes more complex with a professional job, more expectations in your relationships, and perhaps motherhood or other home responsibilities, you are required to row harder and faster. You personally take on the "weight" of more and more projects, tasks, people management, and/or home responsibilities. If you don't row harder and faster, your boat may sink. You are rewarded for your performance and given your first promotion. And then your second promotion. And then the time comes when you can't imagine taking on another thing. You have maximized every second of your waking hours. It is right about this time when we see a massive drop-off of women advancing into higher levels of leadership.

Could it be that right at that moment of potential advancement into increased levels of leadership responsibility and scope, women are exhausted? That we can't fathom more hard, fast rowing? Could it be that when we look at the reality of the next big job, that what we really see, and implicitly reject, is a life of more hard, fast rowing? All the while, the people we love in our lives are giving us the "gift of feedback" that they are worried we are doing too much and not taking care of ourselves? All we know is what we have done to get us where we have arrived thus far in our life: more effort, more time, more personal oversight and time spent = our proven value.

Could it also be that the impact of our "I'll just take it all on myself" mentality (and thus, tsunami-size wave creation) has turned off those who are in positions to help us advance?

Combine the effort we have made at home and at work with a known bias, commonly referred to as "Performance Evaluation Bias" and you have the perfect storm. Performance Evaluation Bias refers to the following: Men tend to be evaluated more on their potential and women more on their achievements to date. To this, please join my fatigued yet intact Inner Critic while she stages an utter revolt: "Are you freaking kidding me? So, Professor Hansen, I would LOVE to 'master selectivity,' but it seems that the world wants to see me do more, achieve more, perform more, to essentially row hard and row fast."

PAUSE. Tell your Inner Critic to please be seated. BREATHE. Cue curiosity. *But wait. Maybe, just maybe, there is a way I can advance into greater leadership impact, and not do it all myself? Why else might I be doing too much? What can I change for myself so that I can run over this hurdle?*

What is fascinating to me, and hopefully instructive for us all, is *why* we find ourselves going, going, going—doing, doing, doing—over-rowing the proverbial boat, and what we can do about it. The truth, I have come to believe, stems from our desire to express our value, or said another way, prove our value. Oh, and we like feeling in control, we like the feeling of a job well done, we like it when it all works as it should, we like when things are done OUR way. This requires our oversight, management, and personal rowing effort. We like saying, "I got this. You can count on me." We like helping others. We like feeling valued and of value.

Marshall Goldsmith, in his international bestseller, *What Got You Here, Won't Get You There*, has made a book title the most powerful coaching concept of all time, especially for women. We women need to fundamentally rethink what we are doing, how much we are doing, and ultimately how hard we are rowing at home and at work if we want to advance professionally. *What got us here* (eager, often perfectly timed and expertly executed rowing) *won't get us there*. Not only are we exhausted, we are unintentionally alienating those around us with the waves made by our too-fast rowing, and/or we are too busy doing it all to see how much willing and eager help we could tap into to help us.

Before I go on to the impact this over-rowing has on those around us, let me reiterate that the discovery of the hurdle of Proving Your Value (like all of the hidden hurdles) is not an opportunity for us to blame or shame ourselves or others. In our home lives and at work, we are supported, affirmed, given public accolades, and sometimes expected to go the extra mile. We women are good at all of this, aren't we? We have been rewarded for this behavior; we have come to—at some level—enjoy the level of importance we feel from being so . . . valuable. Until, that is, we find ourselves confronted with the reality that this hurdle may be hidden *for us*, but it is *obvious to others*.

DATA DOESN'T LIE

The question we ask of women and their rater groups in Linkage's *Women in Leadership Assessment* about the hidden hurdle of Proving Our Value is this: "Does she spend more time engaging, inspiring, and enabling others than on trying to do it all herself?"

On a 5-point scale, with 5 being the highest score (1 = rarely demonstrates, 2 = sometimes demonstrates, 3 = often demonstrates, 4 = very often demonstrates, and 5 = almost always demonstrates), women rate themselves lowest on this question with a normal average of 3.05, and their raters agree with the lowest normal score of the assessment focused on this question of a 3.57. It is not lost on me or any of my colleagues at Linkage that "often demonstrating" a positively worded set of actions is pretty darn good. Having said that, when you look at these scores compared to the others in the assessment, what we see is a not-so-hidden hurdle to advancement. Proving Your Value is much more obvious to ourselves and others than other hurdles. That is, when we're ready to admit it.

In essence, this research question helped us conclude, as a remedy to running over this hurdle, that women need to spend more time engaging, inspiring, and equipping others, and less time trying to do it all themselves. The good news? We're not alone. Think of this as an epidemic of women everywhere over-doing it. A self-inflicted tyranny of sorts that we must admit to perpetuating. Before you slip into a shame attack about over-rowing the boat, please know that you likely *are* inspiring, equip-ping, and enabling those around you. You just aren't doing these things as much as you *could* be—and frankly *need to be*—in or-der for us to achieve gender equity in the leadership ranks. And it also means you are *still* simply doing too much.

HOW I DID IT

Michelle Webb, TEKSystems, On Doing Too Much

Michelle Webb is executive director for the nation's lead-ing technology staffing and services company and *Fortune* magazine's "100 Best Companies to Work For." She has worked at TEK for twenty-two years and now over-sees employee experience. After a long stint in opera-tions, and before cocreating her current charter, Michelle established the company's game-changing office of di-versity and inclusion.

Amidst proving her value at a very loyalty-centered company, where being clear about your own needs and strengths can be confusing, and supporting her family of five, Michelle has often exhausted herself doing too much and not asking for help.

"Perfectionism is my crux. I am a recovering perfectionist like many of us. Constantly trying to get comfortable with being okay, not being perfect. It is my addiction. So is doing too much. I am such a doer, like many of us. I've had to really work on this. I was exhausted all the time because I was trying to do everything for everyone and not making good decisions. It was hurting me because I couldn't be present all the time. It was hurting people around me because they didn't feel valued since I wasn't delegating and trusting them. It's a hurdle for a reason.

"Because I'm the be-all-to-everyone person, I've learned how to make requests, how to ask people for things personally and professionally. How do I make sure the world and the people around me are getting the best of my skills? I allow people to learn and grow themselves or to get engaged. Learning about and practicing the tools that come with the hurdles has given me a structure to think about that in a different way. Now I find less value in getting something done and more in spending time in the right places. I ask myself: 'Am I empowering others around me?' It's life-changing. Proving your value is one of the biggest factors of women saying to me, 'I can't do it all. I don't know how *you* do it all.'

"Today, and because I monitor this hurdle, I get to empower people around me and they get to feel the excitement for what they are learning and growing into because they're getting a chance to be a part of something. But it hasn't been easy, and my desire to do it all and to be considered for greater leadership responsibility invited rumbles. While I have been supported by leaders in my business and seen as confident and capable, when I really started to believe in myself and speak up about the value I offer, I was dismayed at what I heard. 'Michelle is too career-focused.' 'Too focused on herself.' I had male partners hearing these rumblings who cared enough to tell me. Thankfully, many supported me by challenging these rumblings with comments like, 'Do you understand Michelle supports a family of five? Why would she not be focused on a position that matches her capacity? Would you ask a man this? Probably not.' Having this sponsorship has been critical in my advancement. And, while they had my back, I continued my journey of better managing myself.

"Prior to 2011, I was working full time and also as the house manager and 'Webb Family CEO,' orchestrating much of the work having to do with my three young children and household. I had a nanny for my kids, but managed her, too. I could be direct and clear on expectations. Then, when my husband was diagnosed with multiple sclerosis and could no longer work, he became the primary home-maker and care giver. It was a three-year struggle for me of letting him do his new job. *Why aren't you doing it my way?* I had all these ideas of how he could do things, and I was not allowing him to run that part of our life. 'Not doing anything right' was beyond frustrating for him as well as managing the disease that was necessitating he manage our home life to begin with, and I was 'berating' him for everything. It was rough.

"Today, I get to go to work and he manages all things home and we trust each other. Letting go of things being done my way at home allowed me to be fully engaged at my job. Not everyone has this privilege, but it's less about how your system is set up and more about how you negotiate control around all of it. You can choose to let go of control. I was burning out and was not being of use to anyone in a really good way.

"Proving my value and doing too much, reinforced by my desire to have things done my way and my too-high expectations of being perfect, has been a life-changing hurdle for me. Coming out the other side, I am very comfortable relying on my village. The changes I have made (letting go of having it all done the way I want, asking for help) have other people feeling great about what they contribute. Everybody's situation is unique, and my world running over this hurdle is much easier, more positive and intentional for the people I care about at home and at work."

DON'T LET PERFECTION BE THE ENEMY OF GOOD ENOUGH

Don't we deserve some gratitude and celebration for our endless hard work? Yes, we do. And then the party must come to an end. We must wake up and look in the mirror. It was a good ride, and now we need to think and act differently. Do we still need to perform at a high level? Of course! But if we are to step into positions of increased leadership complexity, we must change the way we perform.

We must amplify and leverage the gifts and talents of those around us and think of achievement as a team sport. Even if we don't aspire to a position with greater responsibility, we still risk the burn-out factor. As we age, life becomes more complex (often times emotionally) and doing too much becomes utterly exhausting.

Let's look at perfectionism and how it perpetuates the tyranny of doing too much. I most often see two forms of perfectionism play out in my work with women leaders: The first is when she, after years of honing her skill, believes her work output is better than what others deliver (and sometimes it very much *is* better). The first form of perfectionism comes from a place of being confident perhaps, but usually tilts a bit into self-righteous indignation where she may look down on another (*my work is better than others*).

The second way I see perfectionism play out is when she doesn't want to be "caught" not knowing something or having it "together" and comes more from a place of shame. (*I hope people know I'm good enough!*) Both forms of perfectionism, be that from highly confident women who want things done perfectly or from women who may not be confident, so they insert themselves to be sure everything goes okay, have this in common: They diminish those around them. Let's be clear, in case your Inner Critic is ready to aim and fire at me: there is nothing wrong with expecting great work product. In fact, it is essential. We need to produce great work to be credible with our stakeholders both inside and outside our companies. I'm talking about those who may be immoderate in their "desire for great output or performance."

Note: If you have ever been told you are a perfectionist, chances are your need for "great" has become immoderate and you have prioritized "great" over being inspiring or engaging for the person or persons around you. You can turn this pattern around.

In our Advancing Women Leaders training, after we toss around what this hurdle is, we then roll up our sleeves and wrestle with perfection. One of the hardest things I have seen women grapple with as they think about their leadership journey is the notion that leadership is not a perfect performance. Nor is it about having all the answers. Not even close. I recently was working with a group of high-potential women in a financial services firm on perfectionism and how it perpetuates our over-rowing. One woman raised her hand and told the group the following story: "So, I didn't see this at the time it happened, but recently, I delegated the development of a presentation that was to be delivered to executives. The person I delegated to had two weeks to gather the data and create a deck. The day before the delivery to executives, she sent me the PowerPoint slide deck. I couldn't believe the state of the presentation and felt it didn't reflect what I think is great work. I stayed up all night fixing the presentation so it looked and flowed better. Reflecting on it now, what I must admit is that the presentation was good enough as-is. It was at 85 percent, and I wanted it at 100 percent. My all-nighter not only exhausted me, it also diminished the value and contribution of a member of my team."

What we talked about next was what she would have done differently if she had to do it all over. She came up with her own remedy: "Well, I guess I could have checked in with my direct report along the way to see about the progression of the project, and to share a bit of my own thinking and guidance. Instead, I wanted to deal with this at the eleventh hour and that resulted in a sub-optimal outcome for her and me. I didn't inspire or equip after I delegated."

This is when I reassure her that she isn't the worst manager on the planet and isn't alone in the description of what transpired. In fact, this is common enough that I fondly refer to it as the "drop and run"—as in delegating on the fly, offering no bumpers in the road or check-in's on expectations, and ultimately freeing ourselves as leaders from coaching to the output we would like. There is a fine line between "drop and run" and micro-management. Last I checked, most people don't like either. We want to be simultaneously directed *enough* while being trusted in our own capability to get the job done. This isn't easy for any manager. And it only is worse for those of us who belong to Club Perfection.

TIME IS NOT FOR SALE

When we take on our own perfectionism, starting with a personal audit is time well-spent. To begin, get out a piece of blank paper (or anywhere you can type or write without distraction) and think about the projects you are working on. I follow management guru Tom Peters's assertion that *all work is project work*. Even if the project is planning for a vacation, preparing for a meeting, writing a blog, or scheduling and prepping for a conversation with a colleague. This is your project to-do list. Capture all that comes to mind that requires your time and effort. Making a list may invite feelings of anxiety or be overwhelming. This is normal. Capture as much as you can, and don't just keep it to your working/professional life. You are one person, doing a lot in all aspects of your life. Next, using the exhaustive list you have created, create two columns: column one is for projects that are urgent (require your imminent attention/need to get done in the next day or so) and column two is for projects that are important (require your attention, but perhaps not today or even this week).

If any of your initially brainstormed projects don't make it to your urgent or important lists, make a third list of "projects that don't need my attention and can be done 100 percent by someone else or be left undone." An example of this for me just this week is renewing my dog's town license. I have the form, old tag, and a blank check. My babysitter can do the job. This is the equivalent of throwing something out of your boat—not to sink to the bottom of the ocean, but for another person to take on in theirs as long as it doesn't require *her* to over-row.

Now that you have all of your projects in front of you, pick something you are working on from the urgent or important list that is causing you stress. Write yourself the following letter and share it with someone so you can be accountable to your promise.

To Whom it May Concern:

I, _____, authorize
and give consent for myself to be less than perfect
in the upcoming event of:_____
_____

My attention and effort is required for: _____
_____

I can be good enough (which is less than perfect) at:
_____

And someone else can focus on:_____
_____

Which means that: _____
_____

Signed: _____

Date: _____

Like all behavior change, taking on perfectionism requires we PAUSE between stimuli (OMG, this needs more fine-tuning and my attention!) and response (I must give this my time and attention, or else ...). We need to breathe and take a moment to assess where "good enough" is good enough.

You don't have to know it all. In another recent women's leadership training session, one of the participants admitted to not wanting to "let go" because she deeply believed she needed to know what was going on with all of the people and projects that reported into her. This is a form of perfectionism. It comes from feeling responsible, from wanting to be seen as knowing what's going on and able to step in and help at a moment's notice. For this mid-level manager, not knowing something would be the same thing as falling down on the job. No one ever told her that knowing all that everyone is doing isn't a reasonable expectation to have of herself as a manager of multiple managers who managed others. How on earth could she keep up with all of the work outputs of a large extended team?

While she looked genuinely confused and even fearful of discussing this further, she also knew her "need to know it all" was really beginning to get in her way not just at work, but also at home. Recent feedback in a 360 assessment included comments she couldn't stop thinking about, regarding her being "controlling" and "needing to let go." I decided to ask her a simple question: "Does your manager (a vice president who has responsibility for 200+ people) know everything that everyone is working on?" She stared at me with a blank expression and then laughed out loud, "Oh my, not even close!" I continued: "What does he do when he needs to find out?" She looked at me and said, "He asks one of his direct reports if they can give him an update or find an answer." And then, the lightbulb moment. Everyone else witnessed it, too. She said to the group, "Oh my. I really thought I had to know every answer to any possible question he asked me on the spot. I never wanted to be caught without the answer, for fear he would think I wasn't doing my job. It never occurred to me it would be ok if I told him I would go find out and get back to him until this moment!"

WHERE IS YOUR VILLAGE?

I like it done *my way*. I don't like the word *controlling* because it sounds so awful and so full of blame. It also suggests the person who is appearing controlling is choosing this way of being. Who wants to be called a control freak? Not me. Instead, and given that perfection isn't so much my struggle (my clothes-ironing, never-wrinkled husband at times has lovingly called me "short-cut Susie"), I can admit that my doing too much is largely fueled by my own talk-track which goes something like this: "It is easier if I just do it because I know how I want it done." Or, if I'm being less "service-oriented," it might sound a little less nice such as, "I know how to do it and I know the right way to get it done." The most modest this voice of permission-to-control gets is this: "I don't want to burden anyone else." Why I actually think I, and many of the women with whom I have worked and coached over the years, often have the knee-jerk reaction to do something ourselves is: time.

Frankly, stopping to explain what and how something needs to be done is often more time consuming than simply doing it yourself. And so it goes; the perpetuation of the "doing too much" hamster wheel of being busy.

Being overly self-reliant is the killer of inspiration and engagement. By definition, it leaves others out of the equation. If we are to equip, inspire, and engage others, we need to let them take on work and believe that they will do a great job. We need to let the "bad thing happen"—namely, let some things get done without our fine thumbprint. As a card-carrying member of the Over Rowing party, I knew this aspect of the hurdle would prevent me from leading and ultimately from maximizing my impact.

ENGAGING, INSPIRING, AND ENABLING OTHERS

Enter Liz Wiseman. Liz is a researcher, speaker, executive advisor, and the author of *New York Times* bestseller, *Multipliers: How the Best Leaders Make Everyone Smarter*. In the book, Wiseman and coauthor Greg McKeown look at various types of leaders and identify two different types of leaders, Diminishers and Multipliers. Multipliers are leaders who encourage growth and creativity from their workers, while Diminishers are those who hinder and otherwise keep their employees' productivity at a minimum.

Liz and Greg define "Multipliers" as those who draw out the intelligence within others and enable them to perform at their highest point of contribution. They amplify the smarts and capabilities of the people around them. In contrast, "Diminishers" stifle others and drain the intelligence, energy, and capability of those around them.

What became clear to me as I learned more about Liz's research, was that the unfortunate thing that happens when we women over-row or prove our value (aside from the impact our over-rowing has on our own body, time, energy, and spirit) is we unintentionally diminish those around us. Sigh. Stomp. Yuck. I have done that. I sometimes still do. I never mean to. Honestly, it all comes from a place of wanting to contribute and add value.

Let me set the record straight on this: I have never woken up and gone to work to *intentionally* stifle others or drain the intelligence or energy or capability of someone around me. EVER.

In fact, I fancied myself a highly enterprising and engaging leader. That is until I was the recipient of a gulpy bit of feedback that gave light to the shadowy side of my impact. It was over a casual dinner in a Los Angeles seafood restaurant with a colleague and after a day of consulting. We were alone, sipping a glass of wine and reviewing the success of the day with our client when she said, "Susan, can I give you some feedback?" If a video camera captured what happened next, what you would see is me (eyes wide open and with a slightly forced, but mostly genuine smile) saying something along the lines of, "Oh my goodness, yes, please! I would love your feedback." Inside my mind, the thought that I still recall having was: *Oh, please no, not feedback. Gulp. I was having such a nice time.*

What followed was a discussion that I believe was a turning point for me as a leader, and it has proved to effectively demonstrate the power that Proving Your Value can have on those around us. The feedback my colleague gave to me that fateful night went as follows: "Susan, I want you know that some people in the office are scared of you. You can be really intense and demanding, and they don't want to work with you because of it." I'm not sure if these were her exact words, but I was shocked. If you resumed the video of this discussion, you would have seen me do all the right things: I inquired, I acknowledged and checked my understanding, I thanked her for her feedback, I apologized for my unintended impact, I asked if she had ideas about what I could do to fix or repair with others. What the camera didn't see was my Inner Critic, poised and ready to go into battle.

The conversation inside my head—at the same moment I was nodding, inquiring, and modeling an overall healthy re-action to difficult feedback—was this (read as fast as possible, channel a bit of rage, do this while saying none of it out loud and forcing a smile): *You have got to be kidding me. I just led a strategic change to a business no one wanted to deal with. The leadership team hasn't been aligned on why or how we were in this specific aspect of business, and I helped to clarify it and then was bold enough to change course despite it being an unpopular decision. Further, if I hadn't been managing to deadline, we would have missed our first product launch!*

Then I did what I had started to coach others to do: I no-ticed my Inner Critic, my defensive chatter in my mind, my an-ger and frustration at it all. And I pushed PAUSE. A memory came to mind that made my Inner Critic sit down and stop talk-ing so fast it made my head spin. It was the memory of an-other colleague introducing me before my very first keynote, the one where I acted out my Inner Critic for the first time. Among other really nice things she told the audience about me, she called me a "force of nature." At the time, I recall internally agreeing with this statement thinking, *How nice and yep, that's me! You can count on me to get the job done!* What I didn't think about at the time of this keynote introduction was something I have long believed, but didn't apply to this aspect of my impact: Where there is light, there is also shadow.

And so I did what any self-respecting adult would do, and that evening after dinner with my colleague, I returned to my hotel room and Googled "force of nature" and then clicked on "images." And there it was: a visual depiction of not one, but several horrific storm forces including a tornado, a tsunami, an earthquake, and a blizzard. I sat back in my chair and stared at the images. Oh my goodness. Working with me can be like working in an extreme weather system. I am, in a bad moment, on a bad day when I'm really stressed and trying to get shit done, like an eye of my very own storm. Immediately, I had visions of colleagues in foul weather gear, hanging on for dear life to whatever wouldn't sweep them up in the system that was ME coming their way.

Not to state the obvious, but this is not a winning strategy for engaging, inspiring, and equipping others. I knew then that I needed to slow down my busy, slow down my words, slow down my actions, make moderate my intensity. If I didn't, I would be that "leader" taking a walk alone. No followers. The good news for me is that I had the ability to see the value of the feedback, coach my critic, and take action to modify my impact. I think my family and those with whom I have worked would happily share with you that I am imperfect at all of this, still. I have my moments when I believe I am acting from a place of caring, and yet my impact isn't as intended. It's usually because I am pretty focused on proving I'm right or blasting by someone to get things done. Why? Because I am a recovering, imperfect over-rower.

EMERGENCY! COZY, COMPASSIONATE CENTER NEEDED

In order to manage myself through pretty hard feedback, I had to return to a place of compassion not just for myself, but also for those around me. My own self-awareness has me fairly fine-tuned to these moments of intensity now. I have a good friend who said, "Being human is great; it's what we get to hang all of our mess on." While there is so much truth to that, as leaders, there is an entirely different level of cost to doing too much and proving your value. For sure, it leaves a wake of riptides for all around you to contend with.

Juliet Funt, CEO of WhiteSpace and a self-proclaimed warrior in the battle against reactive busyness, teaches leaders to "de-crapify their workflow." Her research projects that 80 percent of organizations believe their employees are overwhelmed with information and activity, whereas only 8 percent have programs to do something about it. Funt describes a Culture of Insatiability and suggests that a method known as Reductive Mindset is the fix to develop habitual ways of thinking that renounce and strip away the unnecessary in order to discover time to do only the richest of work.

I, for one, am glad that others have a pulse on proving your value and are trying to do something about it. If so many employees are taxed from work alone, I have to wonder when leaders will take responsibility. Chances are they may be too busy proving their value.

IMPORTANCE OF CARING ABOUT OUR IMPACT

Confronted with several interesting (slightly difficult) coaching assignments lately has invited a good deal of reflection for me about how a leader loses the confidence and respect of others. The questions I have been noodling on include: Does the leader *really* care about others? How is that demonstrated? How has it been expressed in previous assignments? Are they too busy task mastering to prove their value and not develop caring relationships with their talented people?

Here is what I have arrived at regarding caring. Caring isn't just being "sensitive" or perceptive or the absence of bullying behavior; it's waking up each day with clarity about why you serve and whom you serve. It's not being obsessed with proving your value so you can free up that time and energy to be attentive to others.

Some leaders want to prove to the world that they can do it, that their value is invaluable. That, to state the obvious, is 100 percent about the leader—and everyone knows it.

In my experience coaching and working and learning alongside some pretty awesome and pretty bad leaders, what robs a leader of credibility the fastest (other than direct lies, repeated horrific decisions, or gross negligence) is when there isn't a consistent and sincere level of felt selflessness in the demonstration of care for others.

Examples of what might destroy the belief that a leader genuinely cares about you are when the leader makes arrogant statements, often needs to be right, dominates discussions, doesn't express *genuine* curiosity in another's viewpoint, doesn't regularly and with ease express gratitude for others' contribution, isn't aware of (or curious about) their impact on others around them, instead of sharing credit is often heard claiming credit or naming past successes, and so forth. And yes, these are all *real* examples.

Popular vernacular calls this "EQ," but it is rooted in genuine compassion for and awareness of others. It is rooted in CARING.

The believability that a leader cares is not always built in large demonstrations (like genuine, heart-felt missives to all employees or blogs to the marketplace, which can be good, by the way), but more so in moment-to-moment acts of grace and kindness to others. *A leader who cares about others has a following.* A leader who cares leaves someone with the feeling that they want to be around, and work for, that leader, not because of the leader's status or title, but because they feel good about themselves. They believe in themselves and their impact when they are being led by that person. Often, this isn't because the leader told them this was true. It is because the leader expressed curiosity, listened, applauded, and encouraged them.

No one is perfect at this. And, it's really hard to do consistently when over-rowing to prove your value. Leaders need to make hard calls daily that often don't please everyone. Caring can be risky business, especially if the human the leader expresses care for isn't the right resource for the job at hand or needs to be told something that won't feel good to them. Firing is the extreme, delivering bad news is only occasional, but developmental feedback can be often.

Lastly, leaders are human and want to be recognized for their contributions, too! All of this makes for what is a simple notion (caring) a bit complex.

Why many give up on (instead of fight for) their leader is usually this: There isn't a belief that, at the end of the day, the leader is out for much more than proving him- or herself. The leader has failed at the inspiration part of the job—enrolling others in the vision of what we're here to do, resulting in getting the hearts and minds and added effort of their people. Enrolling others in the vision has to connect with the follower's purpose or ignite something in the follower. Perceptions of the leader's incompetence or moments of imperfect judgment are no longer tolerated or made up for by followers in the absence of inspiration and felt care for people.

It doesn't mean the leader can't win over others when they need to, can't authentically advocate for someone or something they believe in, or have moments of vulnerability and grace. Yet when these things are the exception and not the rule, most followers eventually quit the leader.

The criteria the Warren Bennis Award Committee established for our deserving recipient at Linkage's Global Institute for Leadership Development (GILD®) are our interpretation of Warren's beliefs on the most important aspects of successful leaders, with some of our own additions. This award was initiated by the late Professor Warren Bennis with Phil Harkins, the cochair of the GILD, in 1999. The committee currently includes: Former *HBR* editor and founder of *Fast Company* magazine and now Mayor of Santa Fe, New Mexico, Alan Webber; vice chairman of Morgan Stanley and bestselling author, Carla Harris; NYT bestselling author, student of Professor Bennis, and USC lecturer, Dave Logan; purpose guru and bestselling author, Richard Leider; Linkage's Sam Lam; and me.

Criteria include: deeply affects others (requires the art of caring), self-aware, collaborative, curious, a risk-taker, courageous, sees the big picture, does the right thing, creates impact and meaning, and brings others along.

Ultimately, we all need to ask ourselves: *Is this a leader worth following?* The answer, I maintain, can likely be found in the art and science of expressing care for others. When we are busy proving our value, often from a good place and with the intent of doing right by others, we run the risk of missing the bus on caring.

MOVE BEYOND SELF-RELIANCE: EQUIP AND EMPOWER OTHERS

The best thing I can offer you in your quest to run over this hurdle, and drawing from the experts mentioned in this chapter and many who were not, are a few reflective questions (along with practical tools you can use for each). They are:

1. Are you letting perfection be the enemy of good enough? If so, where? Why?

   a. Practice letting one thing be done not to your level of perfectionistic standards. See how it goes. Then do it again.

2. Are there people around you at work who you don't value or believe in?

   a. If they report to you, it is your job to either help them up their game or see them out.

3. Are you being selective about what you do? Where and to what are you saying, "No thanks?"

    a. Bravely practice saying no and see what happens.

4. Are you asking for help at home and at work? Are you delegating if you have a team and/or resources?

    a. If you don't have span of control where you can formally delegate, go back up to questions 1 and 3!

5. Are you taking time to show your care for others, not in the volume you DO, but in the way you leave them feeling when they are around you? Have you checked your impact and asked how you can inspire or engage stakeholders even better than you are now?

    a. Tell someone who has done a good job (only if it is genuine) that you appreciate them, or slow down and ask someone how they are and stay for the answer!

6. Are you being gentle with yourself and holding yourself in warm regard, especially if you just read this chapter in its entirety and believe you may have some work to do?

    a. Breathe in some compassion, and know that we are all on a journey of forming and growing as leaders. And for sure read the next chapter—on recognized confidence!

CHAPTER 6

RISK IT:
THE ART OF BOLD

Hurdle: Recognized Confidence

The Big Question

Can I do this?

The Big Lie

I can't do this.

The Big Opportunity

Belief in self.

The Inner Critic at Work on Confidence

One-up: "They/He/She sucks at . . . "
One-down: "I suck at . . . "

What You Must Change to Run Over This Hurdle

- Coach your Inner Critic like your life depends on it.
  Tell yourself you're awesome and human (imperfect)
  until you believe it.

- Know what you want (*clarity*) and your unique value (*branding and presence*).

- Find a mentor who is great at what you want to build confidence in (*making the ask*).

- Dare to be bold and take risks. Exercise courage and willingness to lose something of value in order to gain something of greater value.

- Keep an "I Did This" journal.

WHAT ARE WE TALKING ABOUT *REALLY*?

When it comes to a lack of confidence, do you feel alone as if you are paralyzed in a bubble while spectators eat popcorn and gawk at you squirming in your insecurities? If so, consider this: neuroscientists, psychologists, educators, and sociologists have widely studied the seeds of confidence to determine if it is wholly a quality, gene, skill in continuous development, value, principle, or action.

The studies are plentiful and the stats are staggering: we women simply don't understand how awesome we are.

Authors Katty Kay and Claire Shipman call confidence a science and art in their book, *The Confidence Code*, and make a compelling case for why confidence matters as much as competence.

Kay and Shipman concluded that while confidence is partly influenced by genetics, it is not a fixed psychological state. You won't discover it by thinking positive thoughts or telling yourself (or your children) that you are perfect as you are. You won't find it by simply squaring your shoulders and faking it either. But it does require a choice, which is the counter-action to this hurdle of recognized confidence: less worrying about people-pleasing and perfection and more action, risk taking, and fast failure.

They didn't stop there with this premise, as evidenced by their follow-up book for young women, resulting from an overwhelming slew of requests by parents and teachers to speak at schools and nonprofit organizations about the power and satisfaction of a confident life. Since the release of their bestselling book (and preceding game-changing *Atlantic Monthly* article, "The Confidence Gap"), the authors have created a digital war room on confidence-building. (If you want to see how your confidence measures up before diving into this chapter, take their free, online Confidence Quiz at www.theconfidencecode.com.)

What we know for sure is that our belief in our utter imperfection starts young. A survey commissioned by the American Association of University Women found that a girl's self-esteem peaks at age 9, only to resume its possible lift at age 35. At 9, girls felt positive about themselves and were found to be confident and assertive. By the time they reached high school, fewer than a ⅓ of the girls surveyed felt that way. (The survey found that boys, too, lost some sense of self-worth, but not nearly to the extent girls did.) The way we are often found trying to overcome this feeling of not-good-enough is proving our value. It might be that we focus on being good enough in the performance (effort) department, the likeability (friendly) department, the brand and beauty (pretty) department, or the intellectual (smart) department. But most women look to something to make up for the nagging notion that we aren't good enough.

This is why I believe it is so hard for women to really stop over-rowing—especially at work. If we enable, engage, and inspire others instead of doing it all ourselves, how will we build self-assuredness and feel worthy? Where will that proof of our worthiness come from if not from our personal, hard-won accomplishments? Also, being busy is a convenient way not to feel our lack of self-confidence. We may attempt to sturdy our esteem by proving ourselves likeable, and this may work in some situations but also has downsides. When we need to make unpopular decisions, where certain people won't be pleased, we are faced with a trade-off (doing what we think is right vs. being liked). If we have leaned on pleasing others to esteem ourselves, we are likely to be in a bind that's deeper than the decision, or person, at hand. As if this isn't difficult enough, the Likeability Bias detailed in Chapter 3 is also alive and well.

In Linkage's training to ready women for advancement, and as my colleagues work with groups of women to dig deep on confidence, we often recognize and discuss how we women wound up on the low end of the confidence barometer to begin with. There are prevailing external as well as internal factors that impact our confidence as women. The messages we are delivered throughout our lives—how we are socialized to be "good girls"—makes for navigating this terrain of confidence pretty darn difficult. Externally, you can just turn on the television or open Facebook or Instagram. What faces women is a visual barrage of "if you have, do, wear, X—you'll be ok." What sells something that is fundamentally not needed to survive, including everything from lipstick and designer shoes to "better" cars and photos of perfectly orchestrated parties, is the notion that if you buy into the lure of something outside of yourself that is positioned to bring you happiness, you'll be ok. Said another way, once you have that thing or present yourself or your effort in a way that others admire, then you'll finally live a life of confidence. Girls and women internalize these messages (some implicit and some explicit) and unconsciously create standards to which they (we?) can never live up.

Brené Brown is a research professor at the University of Houston and has spent the last 16 years studying courage, vulnerability, shame, and empathy. She is author of four No. 1 *New York Times* bestsellers, one of which I recommend to all women who find this whole confidence conversation a tough pill to swallow. *The Gifts of Imperfection* beautifully illustrates her own experience and her research about embracing who you are. The subtitle is the basis for where to start: *Let Go of Who You Think You're Supposed to Be and Embrace Who You Are*. Brené points out that, "Each day we face a barrage of images and messages from society and the media telling us who, what, and how we should be. We are led to believe that if we look perfect and lead perfect lives, we'd no longer feel inadequate."

Most of the women's leadership programs developed at Linkage are offered as a differential investment for a select and nominated set of high-potential women. Be it Linkage's Women in Leadership Institute or company-specific longer-term development experiences aimed at the advancement of women, we see those women who organizations believe are their best female talent. And yes, most of the women who attend these events don't really understand that about themselves.

Recently, I was in Spain working with a digital transformation solutions business to kick off a six-month women's leadership experience that included thirty-five women from around the globe. The company leaders began, as events like these often do, by congratulating the women for being selected to attend. At this particular kick-off, one woman raised her hand and asked if the presenting leaders could describe the criteria used for selection. After the head of leadership development explained how and why women in the workshop were chosen (because they are seen as a top performer in their current role, or as a talent who has great potential due to effort or positive attitude or exceptional smarts—usually all of the above), the woman's eyes welled up with tears. She spoke softly, "I didn't know I was seen that way. I didn't understand why I was chosen or why I would be here. I didn't think of myself as good enough to be with the others in this room." She had the comfort of more than just a few of her fellow participants, who, over the course of the days that followed, admitted they felt similarly.

When we launched a different initiative at a North America-based company focused on developing organizational capability in sponsorship, twenty-four high-potential women were selected to be formally sponsored by the CEO and his direct reports (all executives) for 12 months. The head of HR, "Pam," personally called each woman to tell her she had been selected and who her executive sponsor would be. Pam reported back to me that in most cases, the women who were informed began to cry on the phone in appreciation (and shock) of such an honor and investment. The tears were not just tears of gratitude. The tears were also an admission that they didn't understand just how exceptional they were. Some even admitted to not feeling worthy of selection.

The bigger the contrast between how a woman feels about herself and the positive feedback she receives from the world, the more emotional she is when she is honored. I have seen this time and time again. Whenever a woman expresses to me how she doesn't feel worthy of accolade or selection into a differential experience, it leaves me wondering what on earth we can do to help women really understand how awesome they are.

The proof is also in the data: Women continue to rate themselves lower than their raters' rate them across every competency in Linkage's Women in Leadership Assessment. When I am reviewing assessment results with individual women or with groups, I (in jest) say this: "The reason why you scored yourself lower than your raters scored you across the board is either 1) you are a smart assessment-taker, and purposefully gave yourself lower scores to save yourself from the anguish that may come should one of your raters give you a lower rating than you gave yourself, or 2) you really don't know you're as good as others believe you are." Other proprietary leadership assessments (those designed not just for women) show the same phenomenon of women rating themselves lower than both their raters rate them, but also lower than men rate themselves on the same instruments.

It turns out that, in addition to evidence that suggests we women aren't as confident as we should be, men tend to be substantially more overconfident than women.

Bias expert Iris Bohnet has concluded that it is almost impossible for us to assess ourselves objectively. Yet, Bohnet's meta-analysis examining leadership effectiveness across nearly 100 independent samples found that men perceived themselves as being significantly more effective than women did when, in fact, they were rated by others as significantly less effective.

Clearly, the name of the game for women isn't to leap past a more moderate and appreciative level of self-confidence and join the ranks of the overconfident. (Evidence suggests that, especially in the investment banking industry, this "overconfidence" can get men in big trouble.) What we are looking for is a balance of confidence and humility.

The Hubris-Humility Index is a concept invented by University of Chicago political scientist John Mearsheimer and MIT political scientist Stephen Van Evera in order to measure the amount of hubris and humility packed into any individual. To get a high score on the Hubris-Humility Index, which is desirable, it is essential to have large quotients of both hubris and humility. If an individual has an abundance of one quality, but a shortage of the other, then he or she gets a low score. A lot of hubris cannot compensate for a lack of humility, and vice versa. In short, you need both.

There is no excuse any longer! We can't lean on the belief some have that, "I don't want others to think I'm full of myself." We need to right-size our confidence, without second guessing if we are overconfident. Here's how: Philip Tetlock is a Canadian-American political science writer, and is currently the Annenberg University Professor at the University of Pennsylvania, where he is cross-appointed at the Wharton School and the

School of Arts and Sciences. Tetlock is also co-principal investigator of The Good Judgment Project, a multi-year study of the feasibility of improving the accuracy of probability judgments of high-stakes, real-world events. Tetlock solves something with clarity that so many women with whom I have worked struggle with mightily, and solves a foundational riddle about recognized confidence that I suggest we use as our foundational guiding light.

Tetlock says: "The humility required for good judgment is not self-doubt—the sense that you are untalented, unintelligent, or unworthy. It is intellectual humility. It is a recognition that reality is profoundly complex, that seeing things clearly is a constant struggle."

My version of Tetlock's wisdom: Stay curious, assume you don't see the entire picture, and trust that you can, with the help of others, run over this hurdle of recognized confidence whenever it presents itself.

CONFIDENCE VS. WORTHINESS

For the sake of overcoming a lack of self-assuredness, all the signs point to another dynamic at play, which is *worthiness*. This feeling of being unworthy is famous for rearing its head when encountering a potential opportunity, advancement, lateral move, or even scarier place such as the stage for a speaking engagement or presentation. Potential questions that chirp in our minds may go something like, "Why would anyone want to listen to what I have to say? Why spend time trying to land a new position when someone else will get it in the end? What if I don't know the answer when called upon? What if I should have worn something else?"

The unfortunate event to come from all this wallowing is standing in this debilitating energy of lack of confidence when, in reality, you could be enjoying a new threshold or planning the celebration because your certainty is so solid. Notice how powerful either mental place is, and this isn't just about a state of positivity or negativity.

Shannon Arnold, managing director, Compensation and Benefits for FedEx Ground, where she has worked for twenty-four years, has gone through a journey of personal awareness. Several stops along the way have involved the see-saw of confidence and worthiness. Her talk track has been thick with messages about perfection, which she finally distinguished as being a blatant lie.

"I've had people tell me they don't know many people who are as personally aware as I am—I can tell you all the good and all the bad. With that, it was understanding my Inner Critic and what was going on in my own head. A couple of things I had to overcome with my Inner Critic was a belief in falsehood; sometimes falsehoods are blatant lies and sometimes they are half-truths. Half-truths we believe are more insidious and harder to diagnose. One thing that has become my mantra is: Is that true? Why do you believe that is true? Where did you see that written down? I find that many people I know have these false constructs they've created in their own mind around something they think is true, but in reality when you pull those things apart, you realize that is not the case. One specific area I have focused on over the years is deconstructing perfectionism in my own life. I was under this impression for a long time that perfect was important, and over the years, I've come to a place where, in my own head, perfect is a lie. There is no such thing. It is not even a realistic goal. As I recognized that and how insidious perfectionism was and how many tentacles it had in my life, it was a huge driver in my internal critic. My No. 1 strength is achiever, so I have this double whammy that drives an insatiable need to do things and do them well that has psychological ownership involved that creates this monster Inner Critic that is perfectionism. Recognizing this, I was able to give myself more grace and be more gracious to others in recognizing that we are all doing our best every day.

"I don't have to be perfect. That was the kind of lie I was telling myself, that perfect was the finish line. When you are striving after perfect, you're putting happiness beyond the horizon and you're never going to get there. Another recognition I needed to make in my personal journey was that we are always making choices and that happiness or joy is a choice we make every day. Feeling that this is choice as opposed to a burden is very freeing and it gave me permission to feel happy, grateful, and satisfied in the moment, as opposed to it being somewhere beyond that event horizon."

I have to say that Shannon's truth—and so well-articulated—gives me goose bumps because it is so exact, so true. How many us of are missing out on joy hour to hour while tussling with the endless rope to a stopping point that never exists? Lives can fly by in an instant when we are not in the moment, enough and whole.

Confidence is the belief that you are able to do things well. Worthiness is a favorable estimate or opinion of oneself or another. Having both the belief that you are able to do something well *and* a favorable estimate of yourself are required should our confidence be recognized. You build confidence by taking action. You don't build or earn worthiness; it is a belief that comes by practicing a return to loving compassion for yourself, where the critical voices in your head are replaced by warmer, gentler, far more generous self-talk.

Confidence requires that you suspend fear, channel courage, and take risks. Believing in your worthiness requires you build an internal muscle (call it an inner coach) that has your back every step of the way. Taking action even when you are scared and believing in your worthiness must go hand-in-hand. It is also very helpful to surround yourself with people who believe in you, who encourage you, who remind you of your gifts and talents and want you to go for it in life. The name of the game is knowing who you are and giving yourself permission to be you in the world. When you accept yourself and your gifts and unleash your authentic nature, you need to assume two things might happen: 1) The glory and grace that comes from knowing you are *really okay as you are* will feel good to you and be felt and rejoiced by others, and 2) You may find that the external critics are waiting to cast their judgments. Create your inner fortress of compassion, knowing that having confidence and believing in yourself doesn't mean you will always feel comfortable. Also, have others challenge your thinking when they see you playing small; these people will tell you in no uncertain terms that you can, in fact, do whatever you set your mind to.

Chapter 2 is devoted to building the internal muscle of coaching your Inner Critic. This is a moment-to-moment practice where you return to believing in your worthiness, especially in those moments where you have made a mistake or feel vulnerable or your Inner Critic has the microphone and is pointing out all of the reasons why you simply *can't* or *shouldn't.* This Inner Critic coach will help you to begin anything you set your mind to from an internal place of centeredness—where you speak and act with true belief in your worthiness.

What would be possible for you if you believed in Sophia Bush's famous quote: *You are allowed to be both a masterpiece and a work-in-progress at the same time?* Think about that for a moment. You can be a masterpiece and learn and grow and give yourself a whopping break for not being all the things you think you should be at the same time? Yes. Yes, you can.

Your work to create a world for yourself where you feel confident and are recognized as having confidence requires you to:

- Take action. This is much easier when you;

- Let go and brave the risk, which may result in suboptimal results so you need to;

- Fail fast;

- Have a network of trusted and encouraging friends and colleagues at the ready while you run over this hurdle.

- Watch the language you use as you demonstrate your confidence.

- Be sure to document your wins in a victory journal.

HOW I DID IT

United Way's Darlene Slaughter On Recognizing—and Utilizing—Your Confidence

As chief diversity officer of United Way Worldwide, Darlene Slaughter touches many lives. With her awards for workplace strategy and programs to make a difference and uplift numerous individuals, you wouldn't necessarily think she knows what it feels like to stand in the shadows. Here she reveals that she most certainly does, and how specific events in the workplace helped her get confident about standing out in her own way.

"You grow into confidence. When I was young, I didn't have a lot of confidence. I was more of an introvert than I am now. A real introvert. I would not look at people. I didn't want them looking at me. I would not do things because I was shy about gaining any kind of attention. I tried to stay low-key. I didn't take risks to put myself out there. I was afraid that I would feel silly. I went to graduate school and started to come into my own. I was successful from a work standpoint and always seemed to get opportunities. I got a degree in HR and organizational development. My sister-in-law told me I had this ability to make people feel comfortable. I know how uncomfortable it is to be uncomfortable. I know what it feels like to want to have someone bring you into something when you're not sure how to do it. I ended up in a job where I became a voice for other people. I could easily advocate for other people.

In HR, you're always touching other people in their journeys. In grad school, one of my teachers said, 'You are this big person that everyone sees, but the only person who doesn't know that is you. It's not possible for you to walk into a room and not be noticed and not be seen. You need to get comfortable with that.'

"It was very easy for me to be adaptable and stand in the background and not be out front. As you get older, you let some of that stuff go. I took a program in which we had to talk about ourselves at the end. I felt confident about the work I was doing and who I was helping, but when I had to stand up and talk about myself, I had butterflies in my stomach. I felt like I was getting emotional enough to cry. I realized that I don't talk about myself. While I had a level of confidence, I was not using my strength for myself; I was using my strength for other people. That was a moment of being so uncomfortable. I could support other people through that process though. Then I had a boss who told me to go and ask for a position. She said, I think you will be great for this position, but you need to ask the senior manager. I thought, *I have never asked for a job before!* Especially as this African-American woman, there are some things you don't do. She said, 'You need to tell him you want the job!' I walked in his office after rehearsing what I would say. I knew him. He knew me and my work. I said, 'I want this job.' He said, 'What are you going to do with it?' I said, 'I don't know. I just got up enough nerve to tell you I want it!' He said,

'Take two weeks to put a plan together and come back to me.' I did and we talked it through. I ended up getting the job.

"My confidence level has grown since that point. I would still tell you it's very easy for me to stay in the background and not have to be center stage. My big thing at work is trying to build confidence of other people below me. If I'm not pulling people up and bringing them along, what is the point of what I am doing?

"One time in my career, a manager wanted to promote me to a higher level. I pay attention to my instincts. In many organizations, you don't have more people of color in senior-level positions. I was a junior and she wanted to promote me, but I didn't think she wanted to promote me for the right reasons. I took a two-week vacation and did soul searching. *Who are you? What gifts do you have?* I said to myself, *Just be true to who you are and operate in that space and you will be fine. Everything that is for you will come to you.* I was then determined to be myself and do work the way I thought the work needed to be done and how I could be most helpful.

"Once confidence grew, people started to notice that I was different than others in the organization. I was very authentic. I made time for everyone. I was not interested in titles. The secretary was just as important to me as the VP or CEO. I became comfortable with who I was. People saw and felt that.

"I also say yes to a lot of opportunity. I assume there will be benefits. I pay attention to connections and I don't think things happen randomly.

"When you think about confidence and what you have to share, it's wrapped up together. We have moments when we can be extremely confident about a whole lot of stuff, and it only takes a second to lose that confidence. Someone makes a comment, gives you feedback, criticizes you, and we can immediately go into a spiral and lose that confidence. It gets scary because people are not hand holders or necessarily looking at people's feelings in the workplace. It is very easy to lose that confidence. You can go on a series of interviews for other opportunities and then all the sudden, no one is taking your call or every opportunity where you thought you did a great job and you don't hear further, you sit with all that stuff and start to lose your confidence. You have to be mindful of that. We all can better ourselves and get feedback that can make us better, but you have to absolutely be mindful of not losing that confidence that propels you forward.

"Confidence and presence go hand in hand. If you look good, you feel good. There is a lot of power in dressing. I don't mean spending excessive amounts of money to dress, but you have to dress for some things you want. People see you before they actually talk to you. What they see sometimes determines whether they will talk to you or not. Early in my career, I figured that out.

> *People may not know who you are,*
> *but they will know that you are somebody.*
>
> ——————
>
> I had to come with a full deck. When you're ready to go to the next level, you have to look at what's happening at the level above you in order to go to that level."

DON'T FEAR. TAKE ACTION!

Behind those situations where we lack confidence usually rests that pesky thing called fear. My all-time favorite Carla Harris quote (which I typed up, printed out, and hung on my office door with the hope that every woman with whom I work reads it every time she passes by) is: "Fear has no place in your success equation. Anytime we approach a situation—professionally or personally—from a place of fear, we will under-penetrate that opportunity."

"Well, that's all fine and dandy," you say, "but how can I shift my relationship with fear so that I can better seize opportunity? How do I manifest courage like all those people who ... well, look courageous and fearless and ever-so-confident?"

The answer is no more or less complex than this: We just need to take action. Over and over and over. Courage expert and author of *Find Your Courage* and *Stop Playing It Safe*, Margie Warrell, doesn't want us to wait for courage. Warrell believes that, "Action is the most potent antidote to fear, in that every time we choose to act in the presence of fear we dilute its power and amplify our own. Taking action breeds confidence and nurtures courage in ways nothing else can." Warrell says that courage is like a muscle so each time you muster up the courage to step out of your comfort zone into what she calls your "courage zone" you build your tolerance for risk and your confidence for taking more of them. She believes many women let self-doubt call the shots and encourages us to trust ourselves more deeply and act with the courage we aspire to have.

"Fear is a potent emotion," Warrell says, "which is why in today's culture of fear we have to be extra vigilant to discern between the fears that are serving us and those that are holding us back. If we let our fear call the shots, it keeps us from taking the very actions needed to go after what we truly want and to change what we don't.

"Research shows that women are innately more cautious than men. It's why we must be careful that we aren't being over cautious. Playing it safe can provide a short-term sense of security, but over the long haul it can chip away at our confidence and leave us feeling less secure, not more so."

Warrell says that because women tend to doubt themselves more than men, this leaves us less confident in putting ourselves forward. She provided her best advice exclusively for this book.

1. Make your mission bigger than your fear. You are here for a purpose. There are things that will never be done if you don't do them, so trust that you're here for a purpose to make a mark no one else can. It's not just you who'll miss out if you let fear win, the world will.

2. Get comfortable being uncomfortable. None of us want to feel vulnerable, but only when we're willing to do so

can we take the actions we need to discover how capable we truly are.

3. Don't sell yourself short. Women tend to undervalue their strengths and talk down their accomplishments. It's time to stop. Own your value and take credit for your success. You deserve it. Humility is a noble virtue, but diminishing yourself doesn't serve anyone.

4. Fear regret more than you fear failure. Put yourself in the shoes of you at 80 and ask yourself if you would regret not being bolder right now. If the answer is anything other than a clear no, then trust yourself and take the leap.

5. Lean toward risk. Given that we tend to over-estimate the risks and underestimate ourselves, if in doubt, we should dial up our courage and lean toward risk, not away from it. It will spare you the greater risk looking back one day and wondering, "What if I'd tried?"

The best lesson I learned that developed my confidence was when I was a junior in high school and decided to run for senior class secretary. When I shared this plan with my father over dinner one night, he asked, "Susan, why wouldn't you run for class president? You'd be a great class president, you know." I sighed, thinking he just didn't understand, but decided to explain the situation to him. I said, "Dad, my friends and I have it all worked out. Chris is running for president. Bryan is running for vice president. Ellie is running for treasurer. I am running for secretary."

Looking back, this seems to me now a case study for some unwritten rule I was engaged in about social exchange and tribal togetherness. I was happy to trade my potential for greater leadership opportunity for pleasing my social group at the time. Valuing harmony above all else, I wasn't going to upset the perfectly-arranged political power structure of my senior year in high school.

Dad didn't accept my rationale. In fact, he asked me four simple questions I remember still today. They were:

1. "Why do you want to be secretary?" My answer: "I don't know."

2. "Do you think you could be president of your class?" My answer: "I guess so." His reply: "I know so."

3. "Do you want to be president of your class?" My answer: "I hadn't even thought about it, but now that you mention it, I think I might be good at that. But Chris is running . . ." His reply: "So? Run against him!" *and . . .*

4. "Do you think you would make a better president than Chris?" My answer: "I think I'd take it seriously and work hard."

In the end, I decided to run against Chris. We had fun campaigning and asking members of the class for their vote. I recall the final debate: When each of us had the opportunity to address the class in our high school auditorium and make our final appeal for their vote, Chris stood up and his entire visual presentation was a (real) $100 bill. He talked about how, under his leadership, he would raise the needed funds for the end-of-senior-year festivities. He was funny and full of hubris! (I think he would agree.) I, on the other hand, had several charts and visual aids depicting a vision for the end-of-year festivities, and goals and plans about the actions we would take to arrive at the end of the year with all we dreamed possible. While the race was very close, I won.

Little did I know then what I know now. Taking this risk (upsetting the important establishment of the social order of my world) to go for something (the top job of my class) and putting my all in and winning (becoming the proud senior class president) would set a foundation for my own confidence that remains today. I would be remiss not to point out something you may already have picked up on from my story. This experience also provides early signs of my over-rowing. Did I really need multiple visuals to impress my class, to win over Chris? Maybe I did, and maybe I over-did it. No matter, it is an indication of the level of performance I believed I needed to exhibit in order to achieve in the world. It also set forth two realities that you, too, may contend with: being both confident *and* a bona fide, card-carrying member of the Over-Rowing Party.

LET GO

Joanne Brem knows a great deal about building (and re-building) confidence. In 2009, when she was in a one-on-one session with her mentor—nine years into her second career as an executive coach and with four facilitation and training engagements

coming up—Joanne communicated her self-doubt and anxiety about her readiness. Her mentor paused and then asked,
"Joanne, what do you need to see happen to know you are not a
beginner anymore, that you have arrived? Is it a certain amount
of money you have made? How many more clients you will have
coached? There is some bar I am perceiving you have set for
yourself that when you get to that bar, you will know you have
arrived—that you are not a beginner anymore—that you are
ready and will relax."

"I had to have confidence before I developed competence,"
explains Joanne. "I had to take a stand of believing in myself before I could close this gap with an accumulation of competence-
building experience, and understand what difference I could
make and was already making by the nature of my strengths.
You do need some experience, but I had to take a stand with
confidence."

In your quest to gain confidence, Joanne advises you to
check your assumptions about how much you need to prepare
and also let go of your need to control every last detail:

- Prepare, but discern the level of preparation. Ask:
  What is the desired outcome? What difference will it
  really make? A presentation to a group that you have
  high familiarity with will not warrant the same level
  of preparation as presenting to a board or executive
  committee. This links to confidence in that you may tell
  yourself a story about the level of preparation necessary
  to achieve the outcome and be effective. For example,
  thinking that you need to know a specific amount, be

an expert, or have had specific experiences before taking action (all of which leads to over-preparation). In this moment, take pause and discern. Are your expectations realistic? Remember the times when you have taken a risk or done something for the first time, when you felt not as prepared as you thought you *should* be, and it went fine anyway? Turning this last question into a sentence as an option.

- Let go of control. Whenever you don't trust, you will want to control. Whenever you don't trust, you will go into control mode. Trust that you're competent enough. Be ready for the spontaneity of the moment; it's always in the moment that your environment around you will give you everything you need. Trust this. Things never turn out the way you expect them to anyway.

Joanne's wisdom suggests reframing how we think in ways I see women (including myself) struggle with mightily. What it calls for is a belief and confidence in our capacity to surpass any bad thing that we fear will happen if we take risk. Our trust in our ability to meet the moment is greater than the voices of our fear of failure.

I had a mentor once challenge me to "let the bad thing happen" in micro ways as a practice to challenge my own need to control, which ultimately kept me from taking risks, and allowing those around me to take risks. The example that had the most impact was with my daughters. I am wired, as most mothers are, to discern risk for them and step in as I see fit to remove the risk. When they were very little, this was often appropriate and called for. ("Don't touch that, it is hot!") And if I'm being honest, my need to ensure a risk-free environment went well be-yond their physical safety. The part of me that needed to create order in chaos (grabbing a cup that might tip over and spill wa-ter, or taking from my toddler a loosely-held bag that might give way to the contents in it) was constantly in the driver's seat. I even felt pride in my claim to my children that, "Mommy has eyes in the back of her head." I really believed that this "superpower" of mine prevented so many bad things from happening. (For all the avoided accidents and messes that never happened, I want to say this to my husband and daughters: "You're welcome!")

As my girls grew up, this "superpower" turned out *not* to be a lasting winning strategy. And I could tell it wasn't working for my husband, or for those with whom I worked, either. At some level, I was (and still catch myself) controlling my environment to the point that it wasn't fun for me, my husband, my kids, or my colleagues. I became the personal manifestation of anti-risk taking. When we are constantly on edge to ensure that things are "just right," it is a sure-fire way to stifle the important work of confidence-building. While I hardly see myself as a parenting expert, I now apply at home (imperfectly and as often as I can) the hard-won lesson of letting go.

Will my teenager and her friends make a mess in the kitchen when making cookies by themselves and clean up sub-optimally? For sure. Does the experience of not having me lurk-ing to "coach" them every step of the way give them room to do it their way and experiment, helping to build their confidence in baking? Yep. The same applies at work: When I have let go of having things done my way, and instead become curious and encouraging of the ideas and actions of others around me, I see some awesome results. In essence, letting go of control to build our own confidence will allow us to also help the confidence of those around us. It's a win-win.

FAIL FAST

So you take a risk and it doesn't go as planned. How do you recover? My belief, and what I have found after peeling back the "confidence onion" with dozens and dozens of groups of women over the years, is that core to building the muscle of confidence is believing we have the capacity to adjust and make okay whatever the consequence of our risk-taking might be. I liken this to faith: When you take a risk, there is part of you that will need to trust (have faith) that you will be able to contend with what comes your way (expected or unexpected) as a result of the risk.

There is a necessary relationship between taking action that might scare us and knowing that risk comes along with the territory when we do. When the unexpected occurs as a result of your risk-taking, knowing you have the capacity to recover is essential.

The volume of reports from real women about how low the threshold is for failure (imperfection), yet how high the threshold is for success (often synonymous with perfection), never ceases to amaze me. This means our relationship with failure needs to shift from "no failure is acceptable" to "an outcome that is less optimal than I wanted may help me grow and learn." It is impossible to live without failing at something, or said in a less extreme way, it is impossible to live without suboptimal results some of the time. How do you cultivate the tolerance of sub-optimal results, especially when you took a risk and things didn't go as planned? You need to reframe the experience.

Ideas shared by the authors of *The Three Laws of Performance: Rewriting the Future of Your Organization and Your Life* about elevating performance might offer us a clue to how we can shift our thinking and become more comfortable with failure. Let's say you have faced your fear, taken action (thus taken a risk that makes you feel uncomfortable), and now you are living with what you experience as the less-than ideal result of your action(s). Your reality may be the bad thing that your predicted "default future" was attuned to, and that you wanted to avoid. What now? At any moment, you can decide to look at your reality with a new frame. What can I learn from this situation? What would I do differently next time? How might this situation impact my judgment going forward about this specific kind of choice? How can I do better? Trusting that you will emerge stronger and wiser from setbacks allows you to take risks and fail and know that you will survive. Leaning on a supportive network of trusted friends and colleagues will be essential.

Last year, and only several weeks after attending a women's leadership experience led by me and my colleagues, I heard from a participant about how she risked and failed. She felt she was qualified for a job opening at her company that would be a promotion and an exciting next step for her leadership advancement and growth. In our working session, she pulled me aside and asked me what she should do. I asked her a series of questions: Did she have a sponsor who believed the job would be a good fit? (No.) Had she expressed interest to her manager or the hiring manager or her HR manager about her desire for advancement? (Yes.) Had she formally applied for the job open-ing? (No.) Why had she not applied? (She was worried she wouldn't get it.)

I encouraged her to go for it, reminding her that it was a risk unless she had a sponsor. A sponsor, someone in a position of power who believes in you and will expend their political capital on your behalf, is needed when hiring managers might not know of you or your capability. Several weeks later, she tracked me down to tell me that she applied and interviewed for the opening. She didn't get the job. Then, she told me how proud she was that she went for it. I asked if she had regrets and she said, "Susan, this was a big learning opportunity for me. I need to do this more often. It was thrilling and made me feel alive and vulner-able, and I learned so much in the process. Applying put me on the radar of the leadership team, and gave me the opportunity to take a risk and realize I am okay even though it wasn't the out-come I wanted."

DEVELOP A CONFIDENCE-BUILDING SUPPORT SYSTEM

There isn't a hurdle we should attempt to run over alone. Rec-ognized Confidence isn't the exception; in fact, I'm beginning to think it's the No. 1 reason to surround yourself with people who will be supportive. Like much of the wisdom in this chap-ter, there is alignment among the many experts out there on ex-actly what is most helpful (and what isn't as helpful).

Looking back on the role my father played in my life, I realize that his focused intention on ensuring I had self-confidence truly impacted my life in ways I only now am beginning to truly understand. If he hadn't encouraged me to think bigger about my potential (why run for class secretary when you can run for president?), I likely would have played smaller. If you didn't have a dad like mine, fear not. It doesn't need to be a parent; it is helpful if you have a voice of confidence who encouraged you to reach higher as a child, and it isn't too late to cultivate a confidence-building support system.

My father is still the person I channel when I question my own ability. Even though he lost his 16-year battle to Parkinson's Disease in 2008, I channel him daily by asking myself what Jerry would say. The answer I get every time is: "Go for it!"

I have worked hard to surround myself with people who want me to be successful and who see my potential, and who also tell me the truth. My husband, Jamie, can get frustrated with me when he perceives I play too small. On many occasions, and upon lamenting about whatever it is I was experiencing doubt about professionally, Jamie has often asked: "Why wouldn't you just do that? What's stopping you?" It is critical for me, especially in those moments of self-doubt or when the fear of taking a risk looms large, to have someone at the ready to tell me that I can do this. Sometimes what you really need is a push. A push to action (to think bigger about your impact, to make the call, or ask for what you want) isn't the same as receiving encouraging words. As it turns out, those enthusiastic at-a-girls of "you're the best" might not be working so well, anyway.

Affirming yourself, especially when self-esteem is low, is not as effective as taking action when it comes to building confidence.

As described in *Psychological Science* magazine's "Positive Self-Statements," University of Waterloo psychology professor Joanne Wood and colleagues W.Q. Elaine Perunovic and John W. Lee conducted a study that found positive self-statements such as, "I'm great, I'm perfect, and I am lovable," are not as helpful as encouraging action. (Such as being told to just take the first step. Pick up the phone! Send an e-mail. Ask for the meeting. Take action.) The team asked participants to answer the 10 questions in the Rosenberg Self-Esteem Scale. They then separated the participants into three groups depending on how they ranked on the scale. The people who scored lowest on the Rosenberg Scale were deemed low self-esteem, while the highest were put in the high self-esteem group, and those in the middle were labeled medium self-esteem. The people in the lowest and the highest groups were then randomly assigned one of two tasks. They either had to continuously repeat to themselves the statement "I'm a lovable person" for four minutes, or they had to write down their thoughts and feelings for a period of four minutes. Results showed that the people who'd been in the low self-esteem group and were assigned the "I'm a lovable person" mantra felt worse about themselves after repeating the phrase compared to the low self-esteem people who'd had to write down their thoughts and feelings. The team believes the findings resulted from the gap between what participants were told to feel and what they really felt. Repeating empty statements only served to underscore how far they felt they were from an ideal state of mind. The whole exercise made them feel like a double failure.

What this means for you as you build your muscle of confidence is that repeatedly hearing from loved ones or supporters that you are great isn't as effective for your confidence-building as words that encourage you to take action are. It may take just one suggestion, like my Dad had given to me.

Your supporters can help you most, and you can help those you believe in and support most, by giving encouragement to act. One little nudge might be all you need.

SPEAK THE LANGUAGE
OF CONFIDENCE

Alexandra Petri wrote a very funny/not funny missive, "Famous Quotes the Way a Woman Would Have to Say Them During a Meeting," in *The Washington Post* (October 13, 2015), which was sent to me by no less than half a dozen people when it was published. The piece describes how we women use language that doesn't . . . er . . . serve us sometimes. My favorite example from the article:

> *Man* (in this case, former President Ronald Regan): "Mr. Gorbachev, tear down this wall!"

> *Woman in a Meeting:* "I'm sorry, Mikhail, if I could? Didn't mean to cut you off there. Can we agree that this wall maybe isn't quite doing what it should be doing? Just looking at everything everyone's been

saying, it seems like we could consider removing it. Possibly. I don't know, what does the room feel?"

I'm here to tell you that you can take all of the wisdom from this chapter (for that matter, all the wisdom from this book) and couple it with speaking in apologies and other self-dismissive qualifiers and ruin your efforts to run over the hurdles. Mean what you say and say what you mean. No need to apologize for taking someone's time. If you are adding value (an idea or a thought or taking action in some way), OWN IT. I want to coach every woman who I run across (especially in public, at airports or elsewhere) who says "I'm sorry" when they actually mean "excuse me" to STOP IT. Don't apologize unless you have hurt someone and you need to repair. Asking me to please move my bag so you can reach yours doesn't warrant an apology. If you accidentally slam into me while hustling to where you need to go, an apology would be nice. Don't give away your power—ultimately risking how recognized your confidence is by others—by over-qualifying and under-appreciating your point of view.

Please understand that I am not imploring you to speak more like a man. Barbara Annis and her team at the Gender Intelligence Institute tell us that women use more descriptors when speaking than men do. According to Annis's research, we women also prefer to influence and make arguments with stories (ours and others), while most men prefer supporting arguments with facts and data. Knowing this, we women could still pay a bit more attention to our words and refrain from diminishing our valuable insight with the words we choose to use as we share it.

CREATE (TODAY!) YOUR
"I DID THIS" JOURNAL

You have surrounded yourself with inspiring and encouraging role models and supporters. You see the opportunity before you to take action in a way you haven't before—at least not at this moment or stage of life/work/insight. Confidence is about appreciating your abilities and having a reference of this appreciation when you are faced with challenges. To be aware of and document your successful moments will help as you attribute success, not to luck or someone other than you, but to yourself. This is a critically important action you can take if you wish to build the muscle needed to run over this hurdle.

Underscoring its import is the reality of a psychological phenomenon most of us have heard of called Imposter Syndrome. Imposter Syndrome is the feeling that your success isn't really due to your own hard work, but rather is a result of other people or other circumstances. It can appear in the strangest of places and in the most well-intended ways. I'll never forget being prepped for a keynote for a large semi-conductor manufacturing company, and hearing from my host how her boss, the SVP of talent, forged the way for all of the organizational alignment and commitment dedicated to gender parity in the organization. The SVP was to introduce me, and when she did, she spent almost 10 minutes crediting everyone (literally everyone) in the room, many by name, for their contribution to the effort.

Sharing credit is essential if we are to multiply our efforts and lead inclusively. What I experienced from this SVP, however, was overly-crediting everyone else for getting the organization and its leadership to where they were the day I was invited to speak. It was authentic on her part and true appreciation for everyone in the room. It also lacked any hubris at all; it was all humility and all other-focused. After her intro and my talk, I had the opportunity to connect with her. I told her that I knew she had the vision for gender parity for her organization and shared with her how she could have added one or two statements that subtly and with confidence gave herself some credit. One or two "I" statements like, "I want for this company . . . ," would have grounded her as a leader in the force that created what she was appreciating.

Starting a log, a journal, or a document that is for nothing other than your awesome accomplishments and successes is a great way to temper Imposter Syndrome. *You* had the vision. *You* took action. The results were largely because of *your* contribution. Call it the fostering of positive appraisals. Write about the problems you solved and how your solutions made an impact. How did the achievement feel? What other ideas did it spark? Remember, success begets success. There is no substitute for your own recognized confidence. Use the tool in Chapter 7 called "Value Showcase." This is something that can work as you document accomplishments for the hurdle of Recognized Confidence as well as Brand & Presence.

Let's look more closely in the next chapter at your unique value, and how this impacts your brand and presence. Your supportive network will appreciate some specifics from you about what exactly makes you awesome. Let's go!

CLAIM YOUR UNIQUE SUPERPOWERS

Hurdle: Branding and Presence

The Big Question

Do others see me as I wish to be seen? Am I showing up in ways that instill confidence in the areas I wish to be known for?

The Big Lie

My effort speaks for itself, so I don't need to worry much about my brand.

The Big Opportunity

People use their relationship capital to promote you and the unique value you offer.

The Inner Critic at Work on Branding and Presence

One-up: "I don't care what those idiots think of me."

One-down: "I hope I made a good impression despite what I . . . " (*said, didn't say, forgot to say, wore, etc.*)

What You Must Change to Run Over This Hurdle

- Know your unique value. Understand your superpowers.

- Be your authentic self.

- Be strategic about the impression you make.

- Own your contribution. Be clear about what you can shamelessly take credit for.

- Ask a trusted few if your impact is aligned with your intention.

WHAT ARE WE TALKING ABOUT *REALLY*?

"What do you do that adds remarkable, measurable, distinguished, distinctive value?" Over two decades ago, Tom Peters asked readers this question in an article in *Fast Company* magazine titled, "The Brand Called You." Here's the answer I won't accept from you (and I'm venturing to guess that Tom Peters wouldn't either): "I work hard." Nope. Sorry. If you are reading this book, chances are you have and still work hard, and you care about the value you bring to any situation—professionally and personally. This is *known*. We have already established that you are awesome. Your effort and willingness to work hard distinguishes you about as much as it does for every other hard-working woman in your field/industry/organization. So, it's time to dig a bit deeper, get more specific. What makes you awesome? What makes you uniquely YOU?

The quietest the room gets when I give talks about the seven hurdles is when I suggest the following: "If you can't tell me five things (off the top of your head) that make you uniquely awesome, you have work to do."

This doesn't mean you should walk around telling others how awesome you are, with specificity. Let's keep in mind the good research from Chapter 6 on the importance of striving for a balance of hubris and humility. You need to strive for equal parts humility and hubris. Let's remember, being humble doesn't give you a hall pass when it comes to understanding the unique value you bring and stepping into all of it more fully. This hurdle emerged when I realized that most women truly believe their work ethic (the time, effort, and care they devote to everything they do) will get them their next promotion. And yet, when pressed to explain what makes them unique, only wide-eyed blank expressions stared back. So, let's get one thing straight upfront: It is not only okay, it is *essential* for you to know and be able to articulate what exactly makes you awesome. Said another way, you want to be the one who determines what your unique value is, and how this matters to those who are in receipt of your brand. It is also essential that you care about how others perceive you and the alignment of that perception to your intention. Lastly, people will know if you're trying to be something you're not. Being your authentic self (being you) is your best competitive advantage. This hurdle is only present, however, because we women are still shy to "stand in" (own) what makes us uniquely fabulous.

Yes, you are uniquely fabulous, and you *do* bring remarkable, measurable, distinguished, and distinctive value. Let's look at how to home in on this, and get comfortable owning it.

KNOW YOUR UNIQUE SUPERPOWERS

In her practical guide to career empowerment, *Personal Branding and Marketing Yourself,* Rita Balian Allen suggests the first step in defining and identifying your brand is self-assessment. She suggests exploring strengths and areas for development, competencies required and competencies possessed, your personal and professional interests, your values and priorities, and your goals and aspirations. "Time to self-assess again?" you ask. Yes!

In our transitions work at Linkage, we advise leaders to understand first their desired future state (or vision of what's possible), then their contextual current state, and finally complete a gap analysis. The same process applies to you as you examine your brand and presence. The first thing you need to know is the current state reality of the brand called you. How are you showing up today? What is the legacy you leave when you leave the room? How do people describe you to others? The best way to get going on the "current state of your brand journey" is to lean on those who know you.

This activity isn't the totality of, but derives in part from, a known and respected process called Reflected Best Self exercise, created by faculty at the University of Michigan Ross School of Business. Here's the assignment: Ask 10 people who know you (at work and at home) for three adjectives that describe you. Don't qualify or give examples or say anymore. Just ask for three adjectives that they think of when they think of you. If you need to, let them know that you're doing a brief leadership development exercise. Ask people who 1) know you, and 2) you believe like you. Please don't ask anyone who you think doesn't really like you. That might not go so well. This isn't the time to get harsh feedback or be criticized. When you receive the 30 words, categorize them thematically. If you have lots of synonyms, pick the word you like best that captures the meaning of that word grouping. What you will see is a characterization of how you are showing up currently. *Note: I encourage you to keep this simple and even casual; you may wish to ask people—one at a time, not in a group format—via text or e-mail. People are busy, so you'll want to make this easy for them to quickly reply. You want their impression of you, their perception or experience of you in the most real way.*

The true essence of a self-aware leader is to understand that we are all on a journey of maturing and growing. You have exceptional and unique gifts that make you awesome. The reason you need to get curious about how you are showing up to others is to hone the muscle needed to close the gap between your intention and your impact. As with all of the suggested activities in this book, I have completed this one a few times myself. Examples of words that people sent to me are:

- Ambitious. Enthusiastic. Passionate.

- Driven. Fearless. Sincere.

- Presence. Courage. Wise.

- Depth. Passionate. Intelligent.

- Purposeful. Inspiring. Compassionate.

- Ambitious. Thoughtful. Intelligent.

- Vibrant. Influential. Charismatic.

- Energy. Candor. Busy.

- Approachable. Poised. Intuitive.

- Wicked Smart. Charismatic. Leader.

Cue Inner Critic: *"Wait. BUSY? Is that an acceptable adjective? Did he really think that word, over all possible others, deserved prime-time, top-three callout? I'm busy, yes, but can't he see why?"* PAUSE. *"Ugh. I'm still doing too much. I must make this person feel not worthy of my time somehow. He's such a lovely and skilled colleague to me. I am such a jerk!"*

Let's put "busy" aside for a second. It turns out I can safely say that I am seen as smart and driven. These words are fine, and I assume they certainly helped me in my professional journey. They don't, however, distinguish and differentiate my brand and capture the unique value I offer. The other descriptions (charismatic, purposeful, passionate, courageous) are, however, words that might lend to brand differentiation, and thus, are clues as to how I might provide unique value to others. Upon further reflection, and after reviewing the words with one of my mentors, it was this concept of "energy" (how people experience mine) that I decided was likely a differentiating brand identity for me.

We assign this exercise in various programs, and women report that it is a feel-good and eye-opening activity. This isn't meant to be a conclusive or factual exercise, but a glimpse into how you are likely coming across to others currently. What felt exceptionally good to hear? What gave you a smile? What did you find yourself nodding in agreement to or shocked (yet humbled or taken aback) about? This is a glimpse into how others *perceive* you. The next step as you review the words you received is this: What's missing? Is there anything you believe helped to get you to where you are today professionally, yet may stand in the way or be in conflict with how you wish to show up in the future? While I hope my energy leaves people feeling good about themselves when they are around me (and motivated to keep engaging with me), I couldn't ignore the word "busy." I recalled the last time I did this activity several years ago, many of the same words appeared and there was one that stood out and stung a bit. It was from a direct report of mine at the time, and one of her chosen three words to describe me was "hurried." This isn't an opportunity for me to ignore all of the words used to describe me that felt good and focus on the one that caused an "ouch." However, the "busy" and "hurried" words are an indication that the darn hurdles of doing too much and proving my value are still something I trip over.

My energy and enthusiasm about my work can leave me taking on too much, and thus, one of the actions that came out of this exercise for me was to work with some trusted colleagues and mentors on mastering selectivity. This means saying "no" more, even when I want to say "yes," and making asks of people instead of my knee-jerk gusto of "I'll do it." (More on that when we look at the hurdle of Making the Ask in Chapter 8.) When I take on too much, others may feel as if I don't have time for them, or even worse, that I am whipping around and leave them sensing that there is a storm brewing. This matters to me a lot, because who wants to follow someone who makes them feel anxious? This is my work at this stage in my own leadership journey, and something I coach myself on daily. It involves *slowing down*, something that simply doesn't come to me naturally.

Once you receive and examine your 30 words, there might be a word or two that you also wish was absent (like the descriptor "busy" for me). Are there words that aren't there that you would have liked to see? Is there a way you want others to be thinking of you that will be necessary should you manifest what you wish to in the future? Look back at the work you did in Chapter 4 on Clarity. Now would be a great time to revisit the activity suggested by purpose expert Richard Leider on your Gifts + Passion + Values = Purpose. To see what might be missing from the words you received from others, compare your words from Richard's activity to the words you received from others. Do others see you the way you wish to be seen? Are you holding back a part of you, such as a gift or a talent that you captured in your purpose activity? The first order of business, however you choose to arrive there, is to know your superpowers. You have many. Once you know them, it's critical that you get comfortable being your authentic self.

BEING YOUR
AUTHENTIC SELF

Laura was a twenty-five-year veteran of a multinational company when she participated in a small team I facilitated as part of Linkage's Women in Leadership Institute. She was very senior in her company's legal department, reporting to the chief general counsel (also a woman). In a group setting, Laura was on the quiet side, and despite being no taller than five feet, packed a somewhat stern and powerful presence. She was serious, and she was a thinker. When she spoke up, her comments were always insightful and everyone wanted to hear what she had to say. I got the same feeling about Laura as I have about many women who have had a lifetime career in large corporations. There was something she was holding back, protecting. My spidey sense was that Laura had a long history of bringing only part of herself to work. Because I had other coaching and consulting work with this company, I ran into Laura a few times over the year that followed WIL. But when she e-mailed me out of the blue and asked to schedule time for a call with me almost two years after we met, I was surprised. When we talked, Laura said: "Susan, I wanted you to be among the first to know that, as a result of the experience I had with the Institute and other leadership work that followed, and after almost 18 months of deep reflection, I told my boss (the general counsel) that I am gay. My wife and I got married last week after 20 years together and I shared that with my boss, too! I wanted you to know because I feel free to be me after decades of fearing that I would be judged or not accepted, and I can't believe it."

My eyes welled up with tears from the touching news Laura shared. I had suspected Laura might be gay, and she was not at all open to sharing much of herself so there was never an opportunity to speak with her about her private life. Frankly, it's none of my business. But the shell that Laura created for herself only left it possible for a part of *who she is* to come to work and connect with others in her work setting. I jumped for joy for Laura because I could hear how free and liberated she felt. She was still quiet, still an awesome lawyer, and now could also be—at work—a wife to the love of her life. She could bring a part of herself to work every day that she had shut off, pushed down, tuned out for nearly 40 percent of her adult life (the average time we spend at work during our lifetime). If you're wondering why sharing a bit of your personal life at work matters, think of the person you most respect as a leader or who has been the best boss you have ever had. Did you know anything about them personally? Chances are, they showed you a bit about themselves, about what they care about, about who they love. Maybe not—but for sure we are willing to work harder with and for people who give something away that might be personal and seek to connect—even if subtly. People want to be led by people who care and show authenticity. It's not just ok—it's important—to bring some of yourself to work that you feel can help you to connect with others more.

You can imagine my elation when, several months after this powerful conversation and when I was again visiting the company for another project, I saw that Laura was sitting at a table outside the corporate cafeteria sharing leaflets with passers-by about the company's PRIDE week in support of the LGBTQ community. To this day, I feel waves of gratitude for having met Laura, for what she taught me about courage and bravery. I only wish she had experienced more of her life where she was as happy as she was sitting at that table, being her full authentic self. *(If you are gay and have chosen not to be out and open at work, I am not advocating that you run to your boss or others if, to date, you have been apprehensive doing so. This is a choice I would want you to weigh in the context of the people and situation you find yourself involved in. Having said that, I offer to you Laura's story as an example of what coming into your full authentic self can mean.)*

Bill George, in his book *True North: Discover Your Authentic Leadership,* captures the opportunity before us as follows: "Just as a compass points toward a magnetic field, your True North pulls you toward the purpose of your internal compass, your leadership will be authentic, and people will naturally want to associate with you. Although others may guide or influence you, your truth is derived from your life story and only you can determine what it should be."

Authentic leaders reveal their true selves to those around them. They don't hide who they are. This does not mean they share with the world every detail about their personal lives or something that may not be applicable to others. What it does mean is that they are vulnerable and open with others about some of the challenges they have faced in the past or may be currently facing. So, you ask, how do you find your authentic self? Oftentimes, the clues to your authenticity live in the moments when you have found the greatest sense of belonging (ability to be fully yourself around others, utterly accepted, even rejoiced) or when the opposite has been true—when you haven't felt accepted or you have been downright rejected or somehow sense you can't be fully yourself with the people or in the situation in which you find yourself.

A great way to better understand your unique gifts and talents (an assignment I offer to those I coach) is to think about three different times in your professional life when you have been downright joyful. Looking back on your life (and if need be, feel free to go back to early adult life when in school, but if you can, focus on work life) what were the moments or situations where you felt excited to be doing what you were doing, as if you would be doing it even if you were not paid? When you look back, a great way to home in on these moments is to think about the marriage of your internal happiness and engagement, and your external display of that happiness and engagement. You couldn't help yourself but be "lit up." You were *in flow*.

If you can't conjure up three examples, at least find one. If you need help, talk with family or friends who have known you and observed you at different stages of your life. Once you have these moments in your mind, ask yourself: Who were you with? What were you doing? What were you talking about or engaged in? Why was it meaningful to you? Chances are that in these moments, your authentic self was fully unleashed. You felt the absence of constraint in being the you that is the most genuine part of you. Think about a time you had an opportunity to feel open and real with someone at work. Chances are, that person who you were open and real with occurred as grounded and real to YOU. When you open and step into being truly you, you give others permission to do the same. And you also leave others feeling they just experienced genuine connection, which I believe is one of the greatest of life's gifts.

One woman who understands this theme is Amy Bladen Shatto, global head of leadership development at Avanade, the JV between Microsoft and Accenture, two companies with very different cultures embedded in their brands. Avanade was created in 2000 to lead digital innovation of the Microsoft ecosystem of the digital and cloud services. Amy created the strategy for high-potential programs, including one in partnership with the European School of Business in Barcelona. Needless to say, she sees a lot of branding situations and nuances on a daily basis in the fields of STEM, where women are clamoring to enter, remain, and move up. She presses on authenticity as key to your brand.

"One thing I focus on when I am facilitating on leadership development is I always tell participants, do not leave your personal self at the door," Amy explains. "So many conservative companies say, 'Leave the personal side at home, bring your work self.' I always see that as so fake and phony. Bring your whole self and your whole being and let people see what makes you unique. In terms of getting to the next level, consider there may be 100,000 people doing the same thing. It's Amy Bladen Shatto that makes me unique at what I do. Why hire Amy? Coming from Compassionate Center, I am the Amy Bladen that loves animals and travels to safaris to draw animals. I am the Amy married to a Broadway star. I am the Amy that loves musical theatre. All of that I don't leave at the door. I talk about clients and what is relevant, but I also talk about these pieces of me. When you, the tech person, bring who you are, you will get hired as the consultant over others. Don't leave your stuff at home—use it to your advantage. Give it to the organization. Let it help make you a brand. Within reason, bring your personal stuff in. That is what differentiates you. Never think you cannot be replaced. You are replaceable tomorrow, but Amy Bladen, the person inside and who has the experiences in life, is not replaceable."

Amy would be the first to underscore the importance of coming from Compassionate Center, especially when sharing of yourself or being in receipt of someone else sharing of themselves. In Chapter 2, we dove deep into the Compassionate Center. It's critical to work this aspect of managing our inner game, or our outer game—our expression—of our authentic self might come across as if we think we're better than others or perhaps not as good as others. The absence or fear of not being "real" or bringing part of ourselves to work is that others might not trust you and/or can't really put their finger on what doesn't compute or connect interpersonally, but they sense something is overly packaged. Something isn't real. Once again, being YOU in the world must go hand-in-hand with mastering the Inner Critic, or else you might find that you're making excuses for bad or sub-optimal behavior and blaming it on, "I was just being authentic." (More on that soon.)

BE STRATEGIC ABOUT THE IMPRESSION YOU MAKE (TO ACHIEVE YOUR GOALS)

Before joining Linkage, my colleague, principal consultant, and executive coach Madelyn Yucht, deeply researched the questions, "Why, given comparable experience, expertise, and competence, do some people garner more credibility, have more influence? How do some people become the first choice for the next promotion, while others keep getting told they are not ready yet?"

Her research pointed to the fact that people respond to and make decisions about us based on the *impression* they have of us. Madelyn defines impression this way: "How others perceive and interpret *you*." The problem, she found, is that most people do not realize how they are perceived; the way she frames it, most people end up with a "default brand" in that how they show up leaves impressions that they do not intend. These impressions don't accurately reflect their strengths and capabilities.

The call to action: it is imperative to be intentional and strategic about the *impression* one makes. Our aim: to be the most effective, personally and professionally, and to ensure that how we show up and how we are perceived is aligned with our intentions and our goals. To guide individuals through this process, Madelyn developed the Strategic Impression Management Framework, a methodology rooted in the deliberate cultivation of Impression to elicit specific reactions from specific audiences to realize personal/professional goals and objectives. The Strategic Impression Management model posits four key dimensions that give an individual the power to actively choose and cultivate the Impression they make to support their life goals. The four dimensions of the Strategic Impression Management Framework are Distinction, Delivery, Demeanor, and Dress.

- **Strategic Distinction** is defined as your ability to "demonstrate your unique strengths and capabilities so you are recognized for your 'distinctive contributions and impact.'" This is the work we have addressed in this chapter and the chapter on clarity (Chapter 4).

- **Strategic Delivery** is how you "optimize your personal impact; how you 'deliver' what you have to offer in the most effective powerful way." The question asked with regard to Strategic Delivery is: "How can you strategically deliver in a way that gives credit, influence, impact, and results?" What we have found in our work with women leaders—regardless of culture and geography—is that women tend to focus on work quality and execution. What we need to do is balance the focus on work quality and execution with how we position ourselves and cultivate and

Strategic Delivery: Women Concentrate on the Left Half			
Work Quality	**Execution**	**Positioning**	**Horizontal/ Vertical Relationships**
Content	Discipline	Visibility	Executive Relationships
Written Documents	Organization	Credibility	Peer Relationships
Verbal Delivery	Meeting Effectiveness	Leadership	Staff Relationships
Timeliness	Focus	Attitude	Collaboration Skills
Follow-up	Planning		Networking Skills
	Project Management		

(©Madelyn Yucht 2017)

leverage relationships vertically and horizontally in our organizations. *Note: we will dive deeper on the criticality of relationship building when we tackle the hurdle of making time for Networking in Chapter 9.*

It is not enough to just perform your job proficiently—you need to communicate your competency and value to others. Strategic Delivery is how you "promote your visibility and credibility."

- **Strategic Dress** is about "leveraging your personal appearance." While we don't advocate for you to dress in ways that feel uncomfortable to you, we do suggest that you ask yourself some important questions about how your physical appearance may impact the impression you make. Such as:

  - What do you think your Dress says about you— what impression do you think your Dress makes?

  - Does your Dress exemplify how you want to Distinguish yourself?

  - Have you ever looked at how someone else is dressed and thought something either very positive or negative? How do you think it helped or hurt that individual?

  - How do Dress and Delivery work together?

  - Most importantly, in order to achieve your goals (manifest what you want for yourself) and further communicate how you wish to distinguish yourself, how might you choose to Dress?

- **Strategic Demeanor** is how you show up interpersonally, what people see and experience when interacting with you: Attitude, Bearing, Conduct, Mannerisms, Language, and Expression. We need to stay in tune with potential "Demeanor Disconnects"—the things you think you are vs. what others think you are. Once again, as with every hurdle and why the hurdles are critical for us to examine, we want to close the gap between our intention and our impact so we show up in ways that invite others in and get us more of what we want.

Common Demeanor Disconnects	
What You Think You Are . . .	What Others Think You Are . . .
Confident	Arrogant
Cautious	Insecure
Enthusiastic	Doesn't Listen
Flexible	Indecisive
Honest	Blunt/Disrespectful
Strong	Rigid
Passionate	Irrational

(©Madelyn Yucht 2017)

While the notion of being "strategic" about the impression you make might land (as it did at first for me) as the opposite of being your authentic self, this isn't the case at all. The 4 D's are about making sure your *impression* reflects all you are and that your *intentions* manifest in behaviors that match. One could argue that if people do not see us as we intend, our authentic self is actually hidden. Here's why: As you discover, take ownership, and become comfortable articulating your superpowers, gifts, and talents, and as you get more comfortable knowing how you wish to deploy your awesomeness in the world, you run the risk of your behaviors diminishing rather than enhancing others' perceptions of you. You may feel most comfortable thinking out loud and talking through your thoughts and feelings in the moment. You think to yourself: "This is my authentic self, darn it!" However, thinking out loud in meetings can leave the impression that you are scattered, don't have clarity of direction, or are not confident in your own options so have to talk them out. That approach can also frustrate people in a meeting who wish to stay on topic, those who like ideas presented in a succinct manner, and who prefer to get to decision quickly. Your demeanor and delivery style leaves others with the impression that you talk too much or take up too much time or are unaware of your impact.

You may feel most comfortable wearing funky clothing, but if you are visiting a client or working in an environment and the culture dresses conservatively, they may discount you. The message here is that you always get to decide how you want to dress, but you need to be aware that people make judgements about appearance. They make judgments about confidence, professionalism, class, stature, self-care—all of which factor into their impression and thus reaction to you. There is no obligation to adjust, but what is important is to understand that Dress is not a neutral. Your aim is to strike a balance between being your unique self (genuine, real) and adapting to the situation so the impression you make is as you intend. Another way Madelyn suggests looking at the "Dress" element is like playing a sport and wearing the appropriate clothing for the sport you play. You wouldn't go play golf or tennis in a hockey outfit or bathing suit. So, being strategic is knowing what sport you're playing and knowing the appropriate attire so you show up as a superstar.

Belle Linda Halpern and Kathy Lubar, in their book, *Leadership Presence*, offer techniques to develop and inspire presence in ourselves and others. They cofounded The Ariel Group, an interpersonal communications skills training and education firm. Today, Sean Kavanagh serves as CEO and he and his colleagues awaken the spirits of leaders to develop their presence. Sean and his colleagues define presence as "the ability to authentically connect with the head and the heart of an audience (either one person or many) so that you can influence them toward a desired outcome." Derived from the book *Leadership Presence*, Sean shares the four elements of presence we all need to focus on (also known as the "PRES Model™"). They include: being present, reaching out, being expressive, and the work of "self-knowing." Sean describes being present as "really fully showing up—being in the moment, focused on whoever you are interacting with." And is quick to point out what being present isn't: "Thinking about your last meeting or your next meeting or something other than what is happening in the moment instead of allowing yourself to be where you really are."

Reaching out, according to Sean, is all about reaching the other person where they are. "This requires the ability to empathize with the other person's world." The intentional use of language, of metaphor, of story, is what Sean and his colleagues refer to as "Expressive." He says, "Being expressive means communicating in a way so your message will stick. This includes voice, language, intonation, and the work to be done here is to communicate so that you can connect." Your expressiveness needs to be modulated, of course. You'll express differently to an auditorium of people than one on one and you need to be able to turn the dial of your expressiveness and language up or down. (Martin Luther King Jr. declared, "I have a dream," not, "I have a strategic plan.") The last part of the PRES Model is all about knowing yourself, which mastering the Inner Critic and other hidden hurdles requires. The connection with knowing self and your presence is recognizing that knowing who you are and what you stand for, which is often made clear by how we face and overcome hurdles, comes through as you engage with others.

The need to understand your life story, and the importance of this to your brand, presence, and purpose, has been called out by many in the people development fields for years. Whether it is the early work of leadership great Warren Bennis with *On Becoming a Leader*, or Bill George's work years later on *Finding Your True North*, activity after activity abounds on taking time to think about your path thus far. Bill George calls it "Your Path of Life." Warren Bennis called it "Crucible Moments." The Ariel Group calls it "The River of Life." My colleagues and I at Linkage call this "The Leadership Timeline." All of these exercises aim to unearth the same thing: Moments in your life that were turning points. Often these are challenging moments, or moments you learned something about yourself and what you stood for. No matter, knowing your story and understanding what drives you helps as you create your forward journey about what it is that you really want in life. Sean suggests an activity that you might wish to try, while a tad morbid, is to write your obituary. What is it that you want to be remembered for? What is said about *who you are* that makes you most proud? This question will help you as you venture into your life and look at owning your contributions.

If your gifts, talents, and authenticity are your competitive advantage, you must continue to seek to understand who you are and what makes you, you.

HOW I DID IT

Medtronic's Kristy Roberts On Claiming Her Unique Superpowers

Medtronic's aim as an industry leader in medical device manufacturing is gender balance in the workplace and people getting to their full potential. One woman at the center of its leadership is Kristy Roberts, who shares that there is a target to get to 40 percent women in leadership by 2020. (Of course, this thrills me to the core!) At a director level, Kristy manages eight district managers and about 100 salespeople in the field with $175 million of revenue responsibility.

With branding and presence top of mind, Medtronic brought 95 women to Linkage's 2017 Women in Leadership Institute to cultivate emotional intelligence and self-awareness, which for Kristy was critical in advancing her own career path. Here, she describes how she did it.

"I am far more familiar with the part of the Inner Critic that focuses on others—grandiosity—than on me. I go into feeling 'better than' others a lot. My inner dialogue is often: 'Nobody is as smart as I am. These people are idiots.' I go into martyr mode, too. My mother was a martyr and I can see that in myself at times. Grandiosity is kind of fun. You're always smarter! When you come back down, you realize you are harsh on people. I call it my talk track. The more I listen to that talk track, the more I believe it, so I have to change the talk track in my head because it becomes more real the more I tell myself it's real.

"The thing I always have to keep in check is my tendency to be emotionally reactive. As I have gotten older, I have become better. It's a matter of awareness. In the past, it was a development area. I'm very passionate and this passion can sometimes translate as overly-emotional, so I need to watch that.

"By and large, I find that most people don't think about how they want to be known in the organization. Women are so busy taking care of everyone else, they have not stopped long enough to be intentional about how they want to be known and what their personal brand is. When they do, it's usually about results, or at least the women I work with, all saleswomen. But these are highly accomplished saleswomen who make great income and are very achievement-oriented. They are known for their financial performance. The minute you miss a quarter, it falls on that brand. I've always told people to build their brand on more than results. How are you achieving those results? What other value are you bringing to the organization? They hang their hat on the results because they work hard for the results. These women are incredibly supportive of one another. There is a strong bond that they share. This is a very demanding role and there are fewer women in the medical device industry. Those that make it are really accomplished women and many are still doing ⅔ of the housework, ⅔ of the childcare.

"As part of my brand, I was introduced to this powerful concept of mindfulness. I mean, going to the dentist is a miserable thing because I have to lay there and all I can do is think about all the things I should be doing! I just need to lay there and let the doc do his thing, but I can't get up and write anything down. Part of managing my tendency to be reactive and have strong emotions is being at a place where I am rested and managing my stress level. Am I taking the time to take care of myself? If I practice this awareness, when stressful situations arise at work, I maintain my composure.

"Very often, too, I ask if the things I'm doing are enhancing my brand or increasing my equity. Is this a meaningful project or busywork or something that is going to help me deliver on my brand? Women tend to be more detail-oriented, which can be good. A lot of time the devil is in the details, but we also have to be able to see the big picture and be seen as strategic thinkers. I coach women in my company about how to manage their own brand. Not only is this not a bad thing to be thinking about, it's imperative should we wish to make happen what we want to make happen."

OWN YOUR CONTRIBUTION

The time has come for you to write out some of the great work you have done and to own your contribution. First step: Own your contributions with *yourself*. When working with women leaders, there are two practical tools I suggest (that aren't a resume) which help them capture and believe the specifics about their awesomeness (and in writing)! The first *Own Your Contribution Tool* (and this can be designed to share with others) is your "Experience Map." I met Sabreen Dhillon (an up-and-coming leader at Toyota's captive finance business, Toyota Financial Services) after she was selected to attend Linkage's Global Institute for Leadership Development. During our first discussion, it became clear that Sabreen had a bit of a branding conundrum. There was a gap between what Sabreen had accomplished in her career to-date and what people knew about her. It didn't help that Sabreen looks young and she had, at the time, been working in the same department for several years. I suggested she create something that would convey in a one-page snapshot for the busy executive stakeholders she wished to connect with a pictorial overview of her experiences. In a way, this was Sabreen's public and professional version of her Leadership Lifeline. Sabreen came back to me with a very cool and highly compelling image that she agreed to let me share with others. Think of your Experience Map not as a resume, but rather a good credibility-building snapshot of what you have done that you want to be sure others know about. Go ahead; design one for yourself.

Using all of your thinking about your gifts, passions, work experience, and the helpful adjectives you received from others, the second *Own Your Contribution Tool* is a "Value Showcase." This is aimed at spelling out how you add value professionally or "what you bring," and is meant for your eyes only. You can draw from this document in those moments when you feel fuzzy about your differentiation, and certainly before important networking opportunities and job interviews. Think of your Value Showcase as your self-created pep club that grounds you in what makes you unique. Chances are, while your resume may detail all you have done, it doesn't give you an at-a-glance about what you can shamelessly take credit for. Here's a sample of some elements that might go into a Value Showcase and a suggested format for how you may wish to capture it all. Note: This is your opportunity to *brag* to yourself and in writing. Just so you can stay one step ahead of your Inner Critic (or that nasty Impostor Syndrome) be sure to capture examples for yourself for proof that you can unabashedly claim the unique value you capture.

Fun Facts: First Job: Harvesting Grapes • Fav. Sport: Basketball (NBA League Pass) • Fav. Trip: Kenya (Masai Mara, Mombasa, Nairobi) • Most Persuasive: Convincing USC to Accept Me (Age 23) • Most Proud: Helping Raise Siblings • Most Fascinating: Share Bday with Siblings (8-14-77/79/87) • Biggest Risk-Taking: Career Choice, Informing Parents of Relationship, Texas Relo

Experience Map—Sabreen Dhillon

Graduation (BA) University of California San Diego

Major: Economics
Minor: Computer Science Engineering

(1995–2000)

Ernst & Young

Intern (99–00) / Associate (00–01):
• Promoted to full-time position • Gathered, analyzed, and interpreted financial data and market trends

(1999–2001)

Graduation (MBA) University of Southern California Marshall School of Business.

Concentration: Finance

(2001–2003)

RSM EquiCo Capital Markets LLC / H&R Block

Corporate Valuations Sr. Analyst (03–04): • "Rookie of the Year" • Pro forma, DCF analyses, public comparable and private transaction analyses **Corporate Valuations Associate (04–05):** • Promoted after 13 months • Authored 50+ valuations • Interviewed applicants (1 of 2 Associates in Dept.) **Capital Markets Associate (05):** • Financial modeling, one-page teasers, pitch books, and presentations • Attained Series 7 & 63 NASD licenses

(2003–2005)

The Walt Disney Company Parks & Resorts

Bus. Plan & Dev Manager: • Evaluated new business opportunities, market entry strategies, scenario analyses • Led core business assessments and problem solving efforts • CFO presentations and speeches • Inv. Bank analyst monitoring

(2005–2007)

Toyota Financial Services

Finance Strategy Sr. Analyst (08–11): • Developed recommendations resulting in remarketing cost savings of $5M annually in perpetuity • Developed write-up and presentation for winning entry (1st place) in Alexander Hamilton Award for Credit Risk (Grade X) **Finance Strategy Manager (11–13):** • Led development of TFS Business Performance Review (BPR) • Managed implementation of Risk Adjusted Profit (RAP%) metric • Co-managed competitive analysis team (7 team members) • Developed executive presentations and speeches for National Sales Conference, Ratings Agencies, BOD, OBR/OSR, etc. **Finance Analytics Manager (13–16):** • Graduate of ALDP program (GILD, 360 Assessment, Project) • Developed data driven insights to enhance decision-making across the organization (AOGC, ALCO, etc.) • Innovation Award recipient for Retail Actuals • GMA recruiting champion (approach, interviewing, selection) **Strategic Innovation Manager (16–17):** • Completed SuccessShare program (Sponsor: Mike Groff) • Led Uber flexible lease pilot (100 cars) from concept to launch **Relationship Marketing National Manager (17–Current):** • Acquired executive buy-in and managed execution of paperless adoption strategies resulting in expected savings of $11M

(2008–Current)

SAMPLE VALUE SHOWCASE: "WHAT I BRING"

- Strategic and creative driver of growth and financial value: *Creator of commercial viability*
  - Track record of driving top line financial growth
    - Example: Led the business transformation of . . . which led to X% . . .
  - Driver of value creation
    - Example: discerned a need for. . . .
- Visionary and collaborative leader who can execute: *Bringing ideas to action with and through others*
  - Creator of vision for future in how an organization can compete and win; driver of ideas to action by galvanizing others
    - Example: created exclusive . . .
  - Develop strategy and systems and can drive results with agility
    - Example: Developed strategic plan for . . .
- Highly networked and credible brand ambassador: *Igniter of followership*
  - Inspires and attracts talent, channel partnerships and clients
    - Example:

- Strategic Relationship Builder; able to win over others and develop relationships
  - Example:

- Of high Character, Judgement, Integrity, and Purpose: *Inspires and supports others*
  - Naturally appreciative and engaging
    - Example: supported the launch of employee network . . .
  - Great track record of good judgement in a variety of contexts/situations (ranging from internal leadership and innovations to client interactions)
    - Example: often will . . .

ASK TRUSTED FEW IF YOUR IMPACT IS ALIGNED WITH YOUR INTENTION

If pages prior to this one haven't inspired you to think of forming a board of trusted advisors who you can rely on to tell you the truth, now is the time. You will want a sounding board in not just one trusted advisor, but a small handful of people whose judgment you value. These might be what Richard Leider calls "Wise Elders or Wise Youngers" (people who you trust and who can tell you the truth about you, who have some life years and thus, experience beyond your own or have less years and thus, see the world, and you perhaps, through a different lens). No matter what you wish to call them (your "personal board of advisors," your "wisdom council," your "trusted advisors"), take a moment to capture some names of people you can consult with about YOU. Reviewing with these people any thoughts that have sparked for you as a result of this book would surely be some great conversations to have. Specific to Branding and Presence, tap those people who see you in action. Perhaps show them your Value Showcase and share what you want to do more of and how you want to be known. Ask them if they can think of ways you do or don't show up in order to support what it is that you want. Be gentle with yourself when you do; you'll want to be in a place of Compassionate Center as you test out how your brand is showing up in the world, and if your presence is as intended.

First, you'll need to get comfortable asking for help, and this is our next hurdle. Chapter 8 will help you Make the Ask!

ASK FOR WHAT YOU WANT

Hurdle: Making the Ask

The Big Question

How do I ask for what I want if it's just for *me*?

The Big Lie

I can get what I want without directly asking because I am . . . (a hard worker, a good girl, always tending to others, etc.).

The Big Opportunity

Getting what we need and want for ourselves without feeling taken advantage of.

The Inner Critic at Work on Making the Ask

One-up: "He is so selfish, taking advantage of me and everyone around him yet again."

One-down: "I won't get what I want anyway, so why bother asking?"

> ### *What You Must Change to Run Over This Hurdle*
>
> - Build trust. The bedrock of getting what you want is being trusted.
>
> - Start small. Make little asks. Dare to inconvenience someone.
>
> - For big asks, do your homework.
>
> - Be specific about what you want. Get in the right frame of mind.

WHAT ARE WE TALKING ABOUT *REALLY*?

If you don't ask for what you want, can you really keep complaining that you're not getting it? Speaking for myself, I know that I have fallen victim to this cycle (maybe more often than I care to admit). In many cases, I don't want to put someone out, I'm worried that my "ask" might be perceived as selfish, or maybe I just want to do it myself because (at the time) it seems easier.

I have, like many of us, refrained from asking for what I want (and often need!) at home and at work. Putting ourselves last results in everything from annoyance to downright exhaustion and everything in between. So, I recently recommitted to practicing—early and often—the art of asking for what I want. While I don't always get what I ask for (like an upgrade to a seat with more legroom on a long flight), there have been rewards for asking. The least of which is that I'm less annoyed with the people around me who I formerly assumed *should know* what I need, and I bet they are relieved, too, because there isn't as much guesswork about my wants, and I'm not as busy over doing it, only to be annoyed that I'm not getting what I need.

Recently, I had a less-than-ideal reaction to a colleague who didn't provide the information I wanted in advance of a meeting. This is the risk we run when we are not clear and don't ask for what we need and want: Our own disappointment can have an unintended negative impact on our most critical relationships.

We advocate on behalf of our children, our companies, and our families, and yet continue to struggle to negotiate for ourselves. You may sense a pattern here, of one hurdle after the next railroading your advancement. As you run over the hurdles though, you'll notice (and feel!) that skills directly related to a few of these hurdles can help you get better at *asking for what you want*.

Is *clarity* (Chapter 4) setting in? Having a compelling vision for who you want to be as a leader and/or how you want to contribute in the working world will help you stay focused when asking for what you want. Knowing what we want and need in the moment—the "micro requests" that make our day-to-day easier—is critical, too. If your request is connected to something that you are very committed to (or would make your moment more comfortable), you will be less likely to waiver when it comes time to speak up.

Take Maria, for example, who works in a sales field office of a global financial services firm. Her future vision is to work at HQ in a role that will give her more visibility into the operations of the company, access to executives, and cross-functional learning. She is very clear that this is what she wants and why. She needs to find a way to ask for what she wants so that it also meets the interests of her company. She knows her value (Chapter 5), and has spent time cultivating it in her Branding and Presence (Chapter 7).

Do you know what you bring to the table? Are you able to articulate your unique skills, knowledge, and contribution? Can you point to data inside or outside the organization that substantiates the value of your ask?

Let's go back to Maria. Having been out in the field with the same company for more than 10 years, Maria knew what it was like to be "out there" and away from corporate home office. When she heard that one of the company's stated objectives was to include field offices more in day-to-day business operations and streamline business processes, she communicated her strengths in this area to the appropriate stakeholders. In this example, Maria needed to share more of herself ("Hey! I'm interested!") before asking for what she wanted ("Is there a role for me at HQ?"). To ask for what she wanted, she felt deserving, emitting Recognized Confidence.

Are you standing in confidence that you are worthy of receiving what you are asking for? When you believe in your unique value and speak from a place of respect for yourself and others, your power can be triumphant.

Maria had to step in to believing that she is "corporate HQ material"—that she is worthy of being said yes to. And as a matter of fact, when she put her name in for an opportunity that would relocate her to HQ and confidently interviewed for the job, she got the offer. Maria had to share a bit about what she was up for before she found the right time to make her ask. When her hard work landed her an interview for the opportunity she wanted, she asked for the job!

As with all of the practices I share and teach, I imperfectly practice what I preach. Today, if that means avoiding feeling disappointed in myself or someone else because I am aware enough and courageous enough to ask for what I want, then I am making progress. The journey starts with a moment-to-moment choice, and with recommitting to yourself each and every day. It's all about progress, not perfection.

Many women will not make the ask because their fear of getting no for an answer stampedes their desires, particularly when it comes to professional advancement. Comfort zones are real, with a fluffy blanket and pillow to go with them! But this sense of security—and dare I say, apathy—may be coming from a lack of critical thinking around the need and desire. Having a strategy for what lies on the other side of your ask feels concrete and empowering.

Remember Darlene Slaughter's story in Chapter 6 about being given two weeks to design the position she was asking for, giving her a better chance to actually land it? The senior executive wanted to know what she would effectively do in the position before he granted the yes to her fulfilling it. She had boldly gone into his office upon her boss's encouragement, even insistence, but Darlene's preparation and plan not only sealed the deal, but also skyrocketed her confidence to make many more asks thereafter. In essence, we're not talking about just posing a question; we're talking about how to further secure the resounding YES to your desire.

Here's the challenge: The news is out that we women aren't great at this negotiating-for-ourselves business. And apparently, some of the systems around us have enjoyed (and allowed) for this to be the case. The now often-cited and famous Carnegie Mellon University study conducted by economist Linda Babcock found that women simply aren't asking for what they want. The study found that men ask for raises four times as often as women—and when women ask, they ask for 30 percent less.

Babcock leveraged the startling results of the study further and co-wrote the compelling book, *Women Don't Ask: Negotiation and the Gender Divide* with Sara Laschever. They maintain that whether it's higher salaries, better career opportunities, or more help at home, women aren't getting the things they deserve because they're just not asking. The book investigates the gender divide surrounding negotiation, both at work and in the home. Babcock shares: "Years ago, I asked my dean why so many male graduate students were teaching their own courses whereas the female students were more often relegated to the role of assistant. He told me simply: 'More men ask. The women just don't ask.' In the course of researching a National Science Foundation Grant, I found it to be true—women don't ask."

According to a recent survey published by online employer-reviewer, Glassdoor, "Women negotiated less than their male counterparts. Sixty-eight percent of women accepted the salary they were offered and did not negotiate, a 16-percentage point difference when compared to men (52 percent)." According to Katie Donovan, founder of Equal Pay Negotiations, only 30 percent of women bother to negotiate at all, while 46 percent of men negotiate. These figures add up to almost $2 million in lost revenue over a lifetime for the average woman seeking to advance her leadership.

When I am invited to speak inside organizations, and if I belabor the point about women needing to negotiate more when having compensation discussions, I joke I may never be invited back. But it isn't funny. As of August 2017, the U.S. Census Bureau reported women still made 20 percent less on average than their male counterparts. According to the World Economic Forum, it will take 170 years to close the gender pay gap around the world completely. While it isn't just on the shoulders of women to be asking for more, and the work some CEOs are doing to right the pay gap wrong is inspiring (and it's about time), we can't sit idly by. As we dive into how to run over this hurdle, please think about your "asking" in the most focused as well as the broadest sense of the word. Be sure to apply some of the practical wisdom offered to your own pay negotiations.

In their book, *Getting to Yes: Negotiating Agreement Without Giving In*, now in its third edition as a result of its mass resonance (Penguin, 2011), Roger Fisher, William Ury, and Bruce Patton emphasize mutual-gains negotiation, or integrative negotiation in which bargainers seek negotiation strategies that can help both sides get more of what they want. By listening to each other, treating each other fairly, and exploring options to increase value, negotiators can find ways of getting to yes without reliance on aggressive tactics and bitter concessions. Coauthor William Ury is now cofounder of Harvard's Program on Negotiation, where he directs the Project on Preventing War. One of the world's leading negotiation specialists, his past clients include dozens of Fortune 500 companies as well as the White House, where a no or yes could result in dire consequences for the country or the world.

The authors describe six negotiation principles that can apply to every ask imaginable (think kitchen table, boardroom, or War Room . . . if you ever find yourself there):

1. *Separate the people from the problem.* Don't forget that your counterparts have feelings, opinions, and reasons that contribute to what they do and say. Avoid the tendency to blame (big one!).

2. *Focus on interests, not positions.* By understanding what interests the other party has, you may see commonalities that satisfy both you and them.

3. *Learn to manage emotions.* Exercise freedom of expression on both sides. Free expression automatically constructs a safety zone and trust.

4. *Express appreciation.* Words and actions of appreciation build an alliance, even if only for a specific ask. Impasses are much easier to break when the other person feels appreciated for her contributions.

5. *Put a positive spin on your message.* It's very simple: Communicating in a positive way is a much more

effective means of getting a yes than criticizing or blaming. Instead of speaking on behalf of a group (which could feel like a "gang mentality," depending on how intense the negotiation is), speak for yourself only.

6. *Escape the cycle of action and reaction.* The authors introduce a negotiation skill they call *negotiation jujitsu*, or avoiding escalation by refusing to react. Channel your resistance into more productive negotiation strategies, such as, "[E]xploring interests, inventing options for mutual gain, and searching for independent standards."

BUILD TRUST (THE BEDROCK OF GETTING WHAT YOU WANT)

There is nothing worse than feeling like you are being manipulated. Often, this isn't happening because the other person has consciously decided, "I'm going to be manipulative." It is happening because they want something, but they haven't stated it. They haven't been clear or direct in their ask. The thought that I have come across to others as manipulative sends my Inner Critic into a full-on internal war. "Did he really just accuse you of having an 'agenda' as if you are this secretive, conniving manipulator? He can go to hell!" Or, "Oh my, I hope that when I tried to be direct it didn't come across like I was running around the issue just to get what I want. I do try so hard and yet don't seem to be good at this asking thing without people being suspect."

This is a good time to ask if the mere association with asking for what you want sends your Inner Critic into battle. Because, in your mind, you may be perfectly clear about your wants and needs. If this is the case, why the gap between your intention (asking for what you want) and the impact (at times, landing as manipulative to those around you)? I bet you have never woken up, looked in the mirror, and said to yourself, "Today, I shall manipulate." You have, like many, woken up with something on your mind that you want to make happen, get done, drive forward, create momentum around, solve, start, stop, or otherwise rid your life of.

There is a direct association with being trustworthy and being transparent about one's agenda.

The definition of trustworthy is, "Able to be relied on as honest and truthful." Being truthful requires expressing thoughts and emotions in an honest way. It is your ability to express yourself clearly and honestly that will help you get to yes. Your job in assessing the level of trust others have in you is honestly asking yourself how transparent or honest you have been with those very people about what it is you want for yourself. Being a martyr is not a winning strategy. If the deeply held belief you have is that you need to tend to the needs and wants of others before your own, or that you shouldn't ask for what you want for fear that others will see you as self-serving, chances are you have bought into the idea that all of your self-sacrifice should speak for itself. (Cue hand over brow, falling on sword here.) How's that working for you? Chances are, if you stop long enough and assess your situation at home and at work, you have some asking to do.

The first step is, as noted in Chapter 4 on Clarity, getting clear about what you want. For example, let's say you want an hour in your day to go for a walk or to the gym, to journal or read. You want an hour (just an hour!) to yourself. This is an hour a day when no one wants or needs anything from you, you are not catering to another's wants, and you aren't bustling about tending to others. It's as simple as having an hour. Just one. To date, you have told yourself the story that you can't possibly take that hour because of all the things you need to do (for others), because the children need their mama, because the house needs your attention, because work never stops, because all the people at home and at work need your help. Suspend for just a minute those stories, and picture the hour of the day that you would die to have all to yourself. Now, who do you need to ask? Let's say your ideal hour is 7 a.m. and the person you need to make an ask of shares your home. If you're being honest, a requirement of building trust, this ask for an hour will mean the person from whom you are asking will be impacted. They will need to do something different, and maybe be inconvenienced by your ask. Let's pretend it is your spouse who you need to negotiate with, and by asking for an hour, she will need to get the kids up and off to school. (What? No! The kids need ME!) Where things get murky in the trust department is when we contort ourselves to make the other person feel like it's in their interest to accommodate us. Believe it or not, it's okay to inconvenience others, especially if the reward to you is worth the ask and you can pay forward to reciprocate the generosity.

My suspicion is that the ask (which is simple in this example) would ignite trust from your spouse if you deliver it with your intention as follows: "I need to take better care of me, and I would like an hour to myself in the morning. I would like to change up the morning routine with the kids so I can have 7:00–8:00 a.m. to work out/journal/focus on me. What do you think?"

You have just made a request, said what you want and why you want it. That's all you can do. This doesn't mean your spouse (or the person with whom you share home or child responsibilities, as within this example) will agree or support you. It *does* mean that you have been "clean" in your asking. Having said that, when we ask for our own needs to be met, it may open the door for others to ask something of us. It's ok to reciprocate, and it's also ok to say what you can and can't do. No matter, every time you state what you want without demand ("I'm taking the 7 a.m. hour to myself, like it or not.") and without over-accommodating ("I will lay out the clothes for the kids, prep breakfast, and pack backpacks at 6 a.m. so I have 7 a.m. to myself and you're not as impacted."), you just put a notch in your anti-manipulative belt. It's that easy—and that hard. In addition, you may just be modeling behavior they can aspire to; perhaps that other person has a burning ask you can fulfill.

The insight I have about my tendency to people-please made the whole manipulation bit come into clear focus. When I know I want something and it impacts others, removing obstacles or over-rowing around perceived barriers actually does impact others and their perception of your trustworthiness.

Building trust requires that we are clear about our boundaries. I love Brené Brown's definition: "Boundaries are simply what's ok and what's not ok for you." What I see women do, and if I'm honest, what I catch myself doing sometimes, too, is acquiescing to others when, in fact, the whispers in our heart are softly saying, "This is not okay for me." Your work, if you are to be successful in scaling this hurdle of asking for what you want, is to master the art of knowing what is okay and not okay for you. When we know what is and isn't okay for us and we act accordingly, trust takes care of itself in many ways. Our own clarity and courage to act accordingly means that there is congruency between what we want and need (or don't want) and how we show up. This allows those around us to trust that we are being straight. There isn't any guesswork about "what she really wants" or "what she's trying to do."

In her piece, "Brené Brown on Boundaries," Brené is quick to remind us not to think we are trading our compassion for our boundaries. She says: "We want everyone to like us, we don't want to disappoint others.... It turns out, boundaries are the key to treating others with kindness. You can be loving and generous and very straightforward with what's okay and not okay."

Making the Ask means thinking about what is and isn't okay for you. It's this murky and uncomfortable self-examination that is required if we are to ask for (and receive!) more of what we want in our lives. When you don't do this step, you run the risk of continuing to over-row only to eventually feel depleted and resentful, or worse even, wondering how on earth you are living a life that is so lacking in what you really want and need.

Does setting yourself up to possibly be told "no" have your Inner Critic on high alert? She's ready to take down the person who can't see that asking in the first place was hard for you with a stern: "Really? He couldn't just say yes to my very simple request? What a jerk." And/or, she's ready to scold you for bothering in the first place with a nasty: "I knew I shouldn't have asked. My need isn't really all that important anyway." Getting honest about what is and isn't okay for you eventually needs to translate into having conversations with others about it. You will likely feel vulnerable before, during, and after these conversations. If you were comfortable doing this, chances are this Making the Ask hurdle isn't one you struggle with. As with actions you take to run over any of the hurdles, feeling uncomfortable goes along with the territory. The muscle to flex as you venture into asking for what you want is believing in your worthiness. My own courage to ask in more direct ways for what I want (instead of contorting myself or situations in an effort to accommodate everyone and make everyone feel okay while I attempted to eek out something I wanted, but felt somehow wrong in asking for) grew mightily when I began my practice of believing in my worthiness. The aim, in addition to feeling worthy, is to be perceived by those around you as trustworthy. The more you are able to clarify for yourself first (before making the ask) what is satisfactory, and then dare to make the ask of another, the more people will trust you.

As with any muscle you look to strengthen, you need to lift some courage weights and practice asking.

HOW I DID IT

Yasmin Davidds, PsyD, M.C.C., Author of *Your Own Terms: A Woman's Guide to Taking Charge of Any Negotiation*, **On Making the Ask**

Dr. Yasmin Davidds has been in the women's development and empowerment business for 20 years. As founder of a successful women's leadership institute for multicultural women, she receives hundreds of admission applications every year. One of the questions in the application is: What has been your greatest professional struggle to date? Yasmin says that although 95 percent of the applicants have advanced degrees such as a PhD, 99.9 percent of them respond with the same answer—"lack of confidence."

It's clear that self-doubt does not go away with education or achievement. It continues to prevail. She has a theory about this: "No one addresses it." And if a woman doesn't address her self-doubts, it's more difficult to get clear on needs and desires—and ask for what she wants.

Yasmin's own road and rise to a lot of yeses was rather bumpy initially, but she scaled the hurdles to "making the ask" in order to create the life she wanted. Here, she shares some practical insights she gleaned along the way.

Hitting rock bottom tends to bring clarity. Yasmin prevailed time and again, against the odds, to stop being a victim and start living the life she wanted. "I faced abuse, spiraled into depression, and hit rock bottom where I questioned my purpose for living. As I brought myself back up, I had to confront my truth—my reality—and ask God and others for help. Most of us walk through these fires that test us like a rite of passage—and we come out on the other side knowing our strength. My life's work now is a commitment to the empowerment and development of women—to believe in themselves so that they can make the asks needed to manifest the lives they want.

"During my Master's degree work in women's studies, my research consisted of nationwide focus groups in which I asked women, 'Are you happy with the life you have chosen to live?' The results were astounding—and disturbing. Many of the women, especially in my Latino culture, were living for what the culture expected from them—and not for their own happiness and fulfillment. Many of the women were living in a mild depression because they had set aside their own happiness to be 'good girls' and do the right thing, according to others's expectations. Pursuing their own happiness felt selfish. They never gave themselves permission to take care of themselves, build their own self-confidence, and break away from the limiting beliefs that held them hostage from the life they truly desired and deserved.

"There are two themes I see most often that prevent women from breaking away from restricting societal expectations and making the ask—and they create a negative reinforcing loop:

1. A deep lack of self-confidence and belief in themselves.

2. Not knowing how to be their natural selves in an organizational environment where they don't feel they fully belong.

"Years of organizational field research and working with women in leadership led me to conclude that the culture of most organizations is hierarchical—and isn't friendly for women and our way of communicating, collaborating, and connecting. Most women do not know the rules of corporate gamesmanship, which came from the military and professional sports paradigms. Women are never taught the rules of those games. As a result, it is only natural that many women lack clarity about their place in the corporate hierarchy. In our women leadership programs, we examine how women were taught they should be growing up in order to be accepted. Being a "good girl" is always at the top of the list. Now we want women to ask for what they want at the risk of upsetting others or appearing selfish? It completely conflicts with the "good girl" messages and as a result causes ambivalence and internal conflict for many women. Expectations are set at a very early age for women to be undervalued, which translates directly into the pay gap once they are adults in the workforce.

"A famous research study titled 'Pay Allocation' by Major, McFarlin, and Gagnon, asked six-year-old boys and girls to complete a simple task and then "pay" themselves in Hershey's Kisses. The girls consistently paid themselves up to 78 percent less than the boys. This experiment was repeated in middle school and high school with money, and the boys consistently paid themselves more than the girls. This shows how values and feelings of self-worth are set early on.

"Regardless of their origin or background, I believe women can learn how to believe in themselves, be true to their authentic selves, and ask for what they want. This includes embracing their feminine strengths. We can learn to see our true value and what we bring to the table. My life of transformation started when I began believing in myself and reinforced that belief through actions. Going to graduate school, learning and growing, and leaning on others helped build my self-confidence. It wasn't easy, but was instrumental to who I am today. It has inspired me to help other women transform their lives, too. I have seen them do it! They develop into the incredible, self-confident leaders they are meant to be.

"It begins with self-love. It's overcoming being who others think you should be and being your authentic true self. I want women to feel there is nothing in the world they cannot pursue. If they don't go after what they want, it's because they choose not to. It's a choice. Choosing and asking for what we want is the most liberating thing in the world. We can say yes to ourselves, to what we want, and to the kind of life and leaders we want to be."

START SMALL. MAKE LITTLE ASKS. DARE TO INCONVENIENCE SOMEONE.

The rationale I have heard from women who resist making the ask includes, but is not limited to:

- I will be told no.

- I don't want to inconvenience him/her/them.

- They might think I'm not worthy.

- I'm not sure I can do it.

- It won't go well.

- It's not that important to me.

- I care that others are fine, and if I ask for this it might be disruptive.

- I'm scared if the answer is yes that I'll actually have to change my current situation.

- I'm not all that sure this is what I want; maybe I need more clarity.

- I think it will make others angry, jealous, spiteful, passive-aggressive, mean, hurtful, unhappy, etc.

The list goes on. The only thing scarier than realizing you have been operating in a sub-optimal situation for yourself in some way and having clarity about what you want instead is ASKING

FOR IT. When coaching women on asking for what they want, I often find myself suggesting they start with a small ask. I call these "micro negotiations." Here are the rules for micro negotiations:

1. You are asking for something that you sincerely believe costs someone else relatively little time, disruption, and/or inconvenience.

2. You are making the ask of someone who you believe has belief in you and your potential/cares about you.

3. In other words, the stakes are relatively low. We are just looking to practice.

I'll use a simple yet real-life example that just transpired with a very close friend of mine, Jennifer. My husband and I invited Jen and her family for dinner. As expected, her first reply after accepting my invitation was, "What can I bring?" In the past, and for whatever reason, I would say, "Just bring yourselves!" Perhaps I just know Jen well, and trust that coming empty handed isn't an option for her, so instead of a bottle of wine or flowers (which are always thoughtful and beautiful and I ran the risk of her bringing those as well as what I asked—which DID happen), I paused for a moment and thought about what would be helpful. "Can you bring dessert?" her reply: "On it!" This, if you ask me, is a small "micro" request. It required me to slow down and think about what would actually be helpful so I didn't need to shop for or prepare all of the food, and gave her a way to contribute that was genuinely helpful to me. It may seem to you that this is a silly example, and yet how many times have there been opportunities to let someone help (and it would for real be help-ful even if simple) when your knee-jerk reply was, "I've got it, don't do a thing!"

When we begin to ask for what we want, we let others in. Our veneer of perfection and the well-honed armor of "I got this" that protects it comes down just enough to let another in. We also leave less room for our Inner Critic to sing the all-too-familiar song of, "I have to do it all myself . . ." and con-tinue either in a one-up way, "She/he/they never offer to do their part," or in a semi-martyr way, "Thankfully, I'm on top of things enough I never need to rely on others," or possibly a self-assuring yet not-good-enough way, "Well, at least I can host a party well, because clearly I messed up on that project at work today . . ."

Start looking for opportunities to make small asks at work and at home. Could you use 10 more minutes before a sched-uled meeting or call? Ask for it. Do you need to run to the bath-room before a meeting, but don't have time? Stop holding your pee (it's bad for your kidneys!) and tell others you need a five-minute bio break before you get started. Go ahead! Dare to inconvenience someone. Enjoy the rewards!

FOR BIG ASKS, DO YOUR HOMEWORK

For those bigger asks, for example, when renegotiating your work schedule with your spouse or boss or asking for a raise or even a job change, you'll need to plan ahead. In the book *Get-ting to Yes*, noted earlier, the authors suggest the use of "objective criteria" and invite you to, "Concentrate on the metrics of the problem, not the mettle of the parties." They maintain, "The more you bring standards of fairness, efficiency, or scientific merit to bear on your particular problem, the more likely you are to produce a final package that is wise and fair." Please know that the authors want you to take the interests of the other party into account as well, and refrain from haggling over what they call "positions." They explain: "The basic problem in a negotiation lies not in conflicting positions, but in the conflict between each side's needs, desires, concerns, and fears." This means that your No. 1 job is to plan ahead and do some homework. For this, there are two distinct "homework" assignments.

Assignment #1: Find Your Objective Standards

Unlike the wave of work-life flexibility and virtual working arrangements that many companies are adopting these days, you work for a manager that values a "show-your-face/be-in-the-office" culture. Despite this, you have decided working from home a day a week would make all the difference for you. In fact, it solves for the 7 a.m. hour ask because, instead of missing out on the morning routine with the kids, scrambling to shower, and commuting at rush hour to be in by 9 a.m., you can take time for yourself before diving into your day! You are thrilled to have reached the conclusion that this would mean the world to you, and you are ready to book time with your manager and make the ask. It would be helpful to know if anyone else in the company has arranged a "special" schedule. If you don't know, ask around. If you know of an example or two, connecting with these individuals to see what their arrangement is and how they made the ask might be a good idea. Is there precedent for your request? If there isn't inside your organization, do you know of other organizations that have loosened up their working policies to allow for working from home either regularly or on occasion? It would be helpful to have on hand a few companies who have approved such arrangements with their employees (ideally that you believe your manager would see as aligned or similar to your own or among those he or she admires). You get the idea.

For this assignment, find objective data that supports your ask. Do some research. Ask around. Find objective and defensible data that demonstrates an acceptable standard that does exist. Knowing the data that would be most compelling for you to get the answer you want, now turn to homework assignment No. 2. (You may wish to do No. 2 prior to No. 1, but no matter what, doing both will be hugely helpful in your quest for getting what you want.)

Assignment #2: Conduct an Interest Inventory

Get in the other's shoes so they have an easy time saying yes. This is an exercise that first requires no one but you, and will help as you bring curiosity to the discussion when you're at the point of making your ask. It's fairly simple: Make a list of all of the things that come to mind when you think about the other party's interests. What do they care about? What might they value? What fears, desires, concerns, or needs have they shared or have you inferred? If you can, imagine yourself as THEM. Literally try to channel being them and thinking the way they do, and turn the pronoun of the questions to "I." Picture yourself being your manager, sitting where he or she would sit during this conversation, and think, "What do I care about here? What do I value? What are my fears, desires, concerns, or needs?"

No matter your approach, make a list of their interests. Now do the same for yourself. Ask yourself (as you) the same set of questions. Might there be conflicting interests? For example, your manager values fairness, and no one else on her team is working from home. Might there be overlapping or aligned interests? For example, your manager cares deeply about organizational culture and it being a great place to work. You care deeply about the same.

Once you have completed and examined these two exercises, the next step is to develop a list of questions you might have about the other party's interests and get very specific about your request. You also might come to realize you need to do some more research on objective standards; perhaps what you planned to use won't actually speak to the interests of your manager. When you work out a plan, and before you have the conversation, give yourself the opportunity to practice it with someone.

BE SPECIFIC AND GET IN THE RIGHT FRAME OF MIND

As you bring your important conversation (and the insight you gleaned from preparing for it) to a friend or colleague to practice, ask them to listen for the basics: Were you specific enough about what you are asking for? Did you frame it in a way where the other could say yes? Were you generous and trusting (straight-forward, from a place of Compassionate Center; grounded in your worthiness, but no better or worse than others)?

A friend told me the following story, which with all of its clichés, is just about the best example of how we sometimes aren't as specific as we think we are.

> "My husband and I really thought we had 'made it' when we turned the financial corner from taking our trash to the town dump every Saturday to getting it picked up by a professional trash removal service. This isn't inexpensive, and it was a small luxury we once would only dream possible. The initial discussion about who puts out the trash between me and my husband wasn't actually a discussion. But because I carry most of the load at home—most of which we never negotiated (like managing kids' schedules, doing laundry, food shopping, etc. . . .) and we both work full time, I thought putting out the trash was something that he could just 'own.' It was me saying on a Wednesday night before Thursday morning trash collection, 'Hey, can you put out the trash tomorrow?' His reply: 'Uh-huh.' Every week, and with little discussion or conversation about bringing the trash from our garage to the end of our driveway, I would find myself reminding my husband about putting out the trash for Thursday morning pick up. This went on for months. I would think about it on Wednesday night,

mention it to him then and again on Thursday first thing. Earlier in the week if I was to travel away from home that week. One Thursday early morning, with time left for putting it out, I noticed my husband was distracted with the news. So I did what I do, and gave him what I thought was a gentle reminder that today was trash pickup. He turned to me, and in a slightly edgy tone said, 'Yes, I know.' It was at this moment that something snapped in me, the weeks and weeks of reminding and feeling responsible, left me infuriated. He doesn't remind me of MY chores! Then the idea occurred to me that I could talk with him about this pattern, specific to garbage day. But first, I needed to be sure I didn't go on and on, and that I wasn't picking a fight. I had to take pause and be sure I was clear and clean in this request (so it didn't land as full of complaint or harshness or judgment to him). I said, 'Can you please just always remember to bring out the trash on Thursday mornings? Can this be something I never need to remind you of again?' I'll never forget his reply: 'Oh my, YES. I hate when you remind me, as if you assume I'd forget. Assume starting this very minute, you NEVER need to remind me EVER AGAIN and that somehow, magically, the trash will be put out and taken away each Thursday morning.' I decided not to react to his semi-snide sarcasm. Truth be told, it never occurred to me that my 'nagging' was as annoying as me feeling I needed to be his personal reminder."

The reason I share my friend's story is to illustrate how we may just be part of getting ourselves into the annoyances we find ourselves in when we aren't crystal clear about our ask. Of course, this example is also a window into the subtlety of control-freakdom. The underlying assumption when you give yourself permission to be controlling is assuming that without you or-chestrating, things simply won't get done. It's a safe way to feel your personal level of importance, and also a safe way to piss off those around you and keep you in the cycle of doing too much. It also perpetuates possible perceptions that you are manipu-lating. (Hmmm . . . shall I confront this situation with subtle control or overt manipulation?) Wouldn't it just be easier, and cause so much less relationship wreckage, if you asked for what you wanted?

For the little "micro asks" you will need to think in the mo-ment about what you want. For these, taking a moment and consciously slowing down your thinking (even a pause during a call with a friend like I did on the phone with Jennifer) to check in with yourself about what you want is a great strategy. For big-ger asks or lingering frustrations where things might be coming to a boil, it's best to take a longer pause and get very clear about *what you are asking for* before launching into the asking from an emotional state. No one wants to hear complaints disguised as requests.

If my kids tell me they are hungry, I say, "That's too bad." They know what I'm looking for, and it's along the lines of, "Mom, may I have a snack?" or, "When will dinner be ready? I'm starving!" Again, as it relates to mastering your Inner Critic, if you make an ask when you are annoyed with or in judgment of the other person, they *will* feel it. Even if you *say* all the right things. If you make an ask when you are feeling bad, shameful, not good enough, embarrassed, or ashamed, you will undermine your ask. First order of business is to come to Compassionate Center about the situation and the person the ask involves, so you can be clean in your asking. You want the ask that you have become clear about and now you are making to land for the other person as the *request* you are making, not a request plus feedback plus your story about the last six months of your life or theirs and all the feelings you've had along the way. Just ask.

The mounting neuroscience work about the sex differences in the mammalian brain (and the implication for how we communicate as men and women differently) made me rethink how you go about asking for what you want. With Barbara Annis and her Gender Intelligence work as a backdrop, here's the essence of it. As a female,

- You use more descriptors when you communicate.

- You are more inclined to ensure that your listener has a very solid understanding of the entire picture, beyond the specifics of the topic at hand. Context is always important, isn't it?

- You are more likely to make a case using stories (your own and others) and not stick to the (limiting) realm of facts and figures.

Just these three points have given me newfound compassion for the men in my life. Before negotiating for what I want (big or small), I tell myself to "get to the point," and to "Be sure to be extra-specific and clear when making an ask." Frankly, both may help in getting what I want from the women in my life (colleagues, friends) as well, but I have evidence that suggests they are far more patient, and even engaged, when I offer up a story or build on my version of the context of the situation.

Note: Everyone, men and women alike, appreciates being asked their opinion. Part of the job of asking is also caring about where the other person is coming from and getting curious about their take on things. No matter what, when it comes to asking, being specific and clear is essential. Asking in a way others can say yes to requires curiosity to understand how they listen and takes practice, which is a good thing, because the practice of asking is essential in order to run over the final hurdle of Networking. Let's turn to Chapter 9!

BUILD AND LEVERAGE RELATIONSHIPS

Hurdle: Networking

The Big Question

Are you being strategic about developing a network of relationships?

The Big Lie

Networking is a waste of time, and I am better off plowing through my very critical to-do list.

The Big Opportunity

Personally growing from and professionally leveraging a web of influencers, mentors, peers, and/or supporters to help you achieve what you want.

The Inner Critic at Work on Networking

One-up: "Why would I want to build a relationship/spend time with *her*?"

One-down: "She would never make time for me. Who am I in the scheme of things?"

What You Must Change to Run Over This Hurdle

- Understand why this hurdle matters, and return to this understanding!

- Conduct a Relationship Audit.

- Get practical. Create a networking plan.

- Tend to your network.

WHAT ARE WE TALKING ABOUT *REALLY*?

Networking is the process of intentionally meeting people, making contacts, and forming relationships in the hopes of gaining access to such business-related benefits as career advice, job leads and support, useful information on resources and skill development, emotional support, and business referrals. It is a reciprocal building of trust and value. Your network can include mentors, coaches, industry insiders, and those who offer insights in ways that are additive to you, such as realists (truth-tellers), idealists, visionaries, and connectors. The aim, put simply, is to build relationships and connect with others for the purpose of professional and personal growth.

Networking is essential for you and also for others, so they can be in receipt of and promote your gifts and talents. As Juliette Mayers states in her *Guide to Strategic Networking*, "An essential part of attaining one's dreams is the active support and engagement of other people." In previous chapters, it has been noted that the inner circle of your network can be your personal board of directors or your wisdom council—however you wish to think of the configuration of your network. What we know for sure is that actively nurturing relationships with people with whom you share, evolve, and learn is an essential element to your success in your practice of self-awareness and in running over the (often high) hurdles to advancement.

As with the other hurdles, the ease of fostering a network is not a challenge only women contend with. However, the unique added dilemma women have with networking and building strategic relationships (as members of other under-represented populations have as well) is that women may have less access to the majority of those in positions of power. This is not our fault, and it creates an external challenge as we run over this hurdle. I have seen the look in the eyes of mature, professional, awesome women when I ask if they have ever asked to have a conversation with an executive in their company. It isn't a blank stare that I witness; it is pure unadulterated fear. Mayers, also the author of *A Black Women's Guide to Networking,* agrees: "Many experience a deeply rooted fear of reaching out beyond their personal comfort zones." Mayers defines a comfort zone as "that which makes one feel safe," and points out that, "Inherent to the process of relationship building and networking is the risk of rejection, the possibility of failure, and for those whose energy comes from within, the energy drain that can follow networking events."

So, why would you risk rejection and failure just to meet people, you ask? The benefits can be professional as well as personal. Professionally, a well-fostered network can give you access to talent, promotion, wisdom, expertise, and information. Personally, a network of trusted relationships provides friendship, inspiration, clarity, support, and even love.

If you identify as an introvert, please know it's going to be okay. Those extroverts around you may get their energy from connecting with people, but that doesn't mean we're strategic about our time with others. We all need to choose wisely, so "networking" doesn't need to be draining. Nor does it need to happen in large groups or at events, where the overwhelming volume alone can be depleting for many. Instead, shift your frame about networking from one that is about an activity done *only* with large groups of people wearing name tags to one that is about *strategically deciding where, when, who, and how you connect with those you don't yet know (or perhaps build a deeper relationship and connection with those you do).*

In 2015, a study conducted by INSEAD on "Gender Connections Among Wall Street Analysts" found that men reap higher returns from social capital than women. Their abstract is quite telling: "Male and female analysts are equally connected with companies they cover. Connection is associated with more accurate earnings forecasts and more impactful stock recommendations for men, but not for women. Connection significantly improves men's career outcomes such as promotions, but not women's."

We women have work to do with how we think about building a network of relationships, and how we leverage it.

The additional reasons why networking ranks as one of the top seven hurdles can be explained by examining the other six. In many ways, and while running over any one hurdle requires practice running over another, this is the hurdle that is most successfully scaled when you have an understanding (and ideally a bit of practice) of all of the others. This is the culminating hurdle.

Think about it:

- Do you have a deeply held association about networking ("It's a waste of time.") that you need to shift before gearing up to run this hurdle? *Hurdle: Bias*

- Are you clear about what you want for yourself when you take the time to connect with those around you? ("Why bother?") *Hurdle: Clarity*

- Are you willing to put down the oars of your doing too much ("I'm too busy to network!") and make time to network? *Hurdle: Proving Your Value*

- Can you articulate and own your gifts and talents, and give this knowledge to others in a way that helps them help you do more of what you love? ("Doesn't the value I provide speak for itself?") *Hurdle: Branding and Presence*

- Do you feel able to show others your authentic self? ("Really? I don't think they'd think I belong here if I was my true self.") *Hurdle: Recognized Confidence*

- Are you ready to ask those with whom you network for introductions to others, advice, support, and time? ("Why ask for help if I will be seen as weak or inadequate?") *Hurdle: Making the Ask*

With the other hurdles, there is ample opportunity for reading, reflection, and self-directed activities, which are all aimed at boosting your self-awareness and capability in running the hurdle. And you don't want to tackle any hurdle in isolation, so connecting with a trusted few others about what you're tackling has been explicit and/or implicit advice in each of the other chapters. The opportunity presented with this hurdle—making strategic those moments of connection when you network—will absolutely help you with every other hurdle you face. It's the beauty of the reinforcing loop we create when we open our hearts and minds to the very powerful magic of connection. Vulnerable sharing and accepting results is intimacy. Intimacy is implicit in sharing of time, resources, and emotions, such as the Compassionate Center—key to running over the hurdles. Above and beyond these mutual benefits is the feeling that you are not alone. Nothing (perhaps other than honing the skill of deep mindfulness) comes out of long-term isolation. It is a relief to know when others in our peripheral are seeking clarity, building their own brand, or leading up to a big ask. You never know what an exchange of ideas and resources can lead to!

To fully leverage your relationships, it will require that you get a little vulnerable. For some, it might be that the wave of vulnerability comes with making the ask to connect with another in the first place. For others, the vulnerable part isn't asking for the meeting or call, or even explaining what it is you are hoping to learn/get out of the connection; it lies in the moment you allow that well-honed veneer of perfection to fall and reveal the real you. Oh, the possibilities!

Most high-potential career women I have worked with tend not to think of themselves as "networkers," but *do* think of themselves as someone who likes people and likes getting to know and stay in touch with others. One of the most obvious ways networking has helped women is with job placement. For me, and in my near 25 years in the working world, every job I have had has come through someone I know (or someone I know who knew someone else who knew someone else)—not through recruiters or "blind" applications. That's pretty powerful! And it works both ways—I have enjoyed finding (and hiring) terrific talent through my own personal and professional networks. And fear not. You may be thinking you don't have a network, so how can you possibly find talent. Stay with me. You have more of a network than you think you do. You just haven't leveraged it yet.

How we do anything is how we do everything. The "hand" that we extend to others is a reflection of who we are. Networking— meeting and connecting with others—is a great way to "live into" your personal brand. It forces you to think about yourself. What are you about? What do you want others to know about you? Networking can help you to further refine the answers to these questions, and it can help you to manifest the truth of your answers as well. It also allows you to give of your gifts to others, often the most gratifying of moments.

Stephanie Roemer, who is a director of diversity and inclusion at Freddie Mac, claims to have been a non-networker for many years, which is hard to believe since, in her role, she both attends and suggests that women attend learning events in part to *connect*. She's also the first-generation Latina in her family who went to college and then into the corporate world.

"I didn't know what my options were," Stephanie explains. "Fairly early in my career, I didn't have my own family, so I worked extremely hard and long, but that goes to proving your value and being a key player. It worked to my advantage, but it also set a tone in feeling that is what I had to do to perform. I've been at Freddie Mac for 17 years. I worked as a contractor for a year and then came on fulltime. Within a year, I was asked to be a manager. I pushed for myself, but I did not network or understand the value of networking. I stayed a manager and then ended up going to HR and diversity. I stayed at a manager level for 12 years. At one time, I had been out of college for three years and two directors were willing to coach and mentor this guy fresh out of college. He understood making the ask and networking, and I did not. We each had very different experiences in that role as a result of how we connected and why we connected with others. That was the cost for me of being a non-networker."

Fast-forward to Stephanie's manicured networking landscape today. "I just kicked off a program for director- and manager-level women about what a sponsor is and the value of having a sponsor, how they are different from a mentor, and what you need to do to prepare yourself to be sponsor-able. They asked me, 'How do you find these sponsors?' You connect! Make an effort to have coffee or lunch, make inroads to connect across your own division and outside the company. It doesn't mean you have to go to happy hour every day, but coffee, lunch, popping in their office for 30 minutes, follow-up. These were my own challenges, but I get it done."

Stephanie's story is one that represents so many like it. To illustrate further, and while most women I know are good at the art of connecting generally, I have witnessed, on many occasions, women connecting with other women yet without a trace of strategy. An example was when my travels took me to one of our biggest airports in the U.S., the Hartsfield-Jackson Atlanta International Airport. If you have been to it, chances are you too exited your gate only to ride a fair distance in the airport tram to the baggage claim and exit area. On this particular trip, I overheard the following conversation between two women, strangers, both dressed in professional work clothing: "Do you live in Atlanta?" said one woman to the other. "Yes, must get home in time for afterschool pick-up!" The other woman paused, "How many kids do you have?" The reply: "I have three. Ages 4, 6, and 9. Where do you live?"

And the conversation went from there. These women exchanged names and ages of their children, where they lived, how long they lived in the state of Georgia, even where they got married. When the tram reached its destination, they waved and parted ways. My internal dialogue at the time overhearing this exchange was, *How nice!* (I will admit to having similar discussions myself with strangers.) Upon reflection, however, I now look back and think, *What a total missed opportunity.* These women parted ways not knowing where each other worked, why they were traveling, or what they did for a living. I can't help but note how I imagine two businessmen might converse in the same situation: "Where do you work?" says one man to the other. The other tells him and replies, "Where do you work?" The two men continue to briefly discuss what they do for a living, and before the tram arrives at its final destination, cards have been exchanged and promises of connecting on LinkedIn have been made. Now, if the two men end up tapping each other to sell to one another, network with one another, or in general to stay in contact, it's another story. But they at least *could* if they so choose.

I have been guilty of a few common bad habits when it comes to networking. Most notably, collecting business cards along my travels and never knowing exactly what to do with them. With LinkedIn, I am now sure to connect as soon as possible. This is a minor step in the right direction: At least I'm "housing" my connections in a way. I could find the person again should I wish to reach out. But I'm not necessarily leveraging these relationships thoughtfully. Sally Helgesen and Marshall Goldsmith devote an entire chapter of their book, *How Women Rise,* to leveraging relationships. My capacity for meeting and connecting with lots of people is high. My skill and practice in leveraging these relationships thoughtfully needed work. In the past three years, I have been much more aware of my own apprehension to "use" a connection in a way that seems self-serving.

Yet (and Sally and Marshall would agree), changing my frame from one that makes "leveraging relationships" a naughty and bad thing to one that fuels reciprocity and allows me to help others and allows others to help me, has been game-changing.

Who is in your network who you've had passing thoughts of, *Gee, I would love to pick her brain*, yet you haven't? My job gives me unique access to brilliant thought leaders and experts in my field, and to executives and leaders who work in the biggest organizations in the world. I credit reframing my own bias about leveraging these relationships as the single most powerful accelerator to accomplishing my goal of helping other women advance. As with many dreams and goals, I would need the wisdom, support, encouragement, and connections of my vast network. I have been on an extended journey of practicing the ask for help from others. What it required was for me to first be clear about what I needed, having the confidence to make the ask, and being very conscious of how, if at all, I can reciprocate the thoughtful engagement so many have afforded me along the way. It is this generosity of spirit that helps me leverage and continue to build my network. If I can help others, I'd like to. As Sonya Jacobs points out, every relationship needs to be nurtured.

HOW I DID IT

Michigan Medicine's Sonya Jacobs
On Networking

Sonya Jacobs climbed the HR ranks, and in 2016, landed her "dream job" as the University of Michigan's first chief organizational learning officer. Her role consists of programs and strategies to build the professional capabilities of faculty and staff by overseeing the diversity, equity, and inclusion training and education program and Learning & Professional Development in University Human Resources, along with the Medical School's Faculty Career Development program.

What does networking mean to her? "A wealth of mentors and coaches available to me—people who have a great interest in my success." Sonya understands the significance of keen alliances, and that every relationship must be nurtured. Here, she talks about mastering this common hurdle.

"As I grew into more leadership roles, the need for me to be able to show my value and credibility increased with interactions with faculty, physicians, and surgeons. I know my field. I have expertise in the field of organizational development. They have their specialties. I don't tell them how to perform surgeries, but together we can accomplish goals if we have mutual respect for one another and our complementary skills.

"If I don't have what is required, I have an abundance of resources available to me to offset any shortcoming I think I might have. I have been fortunate enough to build social capital, a term I wasn't even familiar with until a mentor enlightened me. I earned that social capital by being available, being a resource to others, and I can call on any of them in my network for support.

"Build networks, build a diverse portfolio of mentors. Have coaching. Get sponsorship. Throughout all of those different interactions, I have been very fortunate to have expertise and support available to me. It wasn't always easy. When I was doing research for my master's thesis, my focus was, and has always been, around the advancement of women in academic medicine and health care, and particularly looking at challenges and barriers that women and underrepresented minorities face when they choose a career in executive leadership in this industry. The research suggested that women of color in particular weren't given feedback because there was a fear of how we would receive it. I had been told a number of years ago by a mentor, who is still a mentor and dear friend of mine today, that I would have to be explicit about seeking feedback. Knowing that, I have always tried to make it a point to seek feedback, but the stereotype is that black women don't want to receive it or might get angry (the angry black woman syndrome, whatever you want to label it). That stereotype exists! I have had to be very intentional about seeking feedback throughout my career. Feedback is a gift, and I have recognized that it is up to me what I do with it.

"The other bias and/or hurdle I faced early in my career was: There was a leadership position that I thought would be my next step in my leadership journey, and I had a significant amount of leader support for that. There were several leaders across the organization telling me:

'Sonya, you should go for this. You're doing a lot of this already.' But I had a colleague/interim director who was in the ear of the senior leader making the decision. I was viewed as being too politically connected for that role. I never thought that being politically savvy or having an accumulation of social capital could have a downside. That was a bias I had to face, and I was challenged to use it to my advantage. They were able at that particular time to say I was not qualified because I had not finished my master's and that was going to be required for the new role. I used that as an incentive and fuel to finish my master's and I did so with honors, so there would not be the potential to use that against me in the future. I am now in a significantly higher leadership role than the advising individual.

"People have those biases and perceptions and they own that. It's real to them, so as women, and as leaders, we have to understand they exist. It's what we choose to do about it that makes the difference. I have to go about trying to change that stereotype. I have to go about understanding why one has bias and help them understand that's not the case, but I can't do anything if I don't know that it exists. I was in a position where people told me of others' biases and I am forever grateful. That goes back to the value of social capital.

"As a result of the networks I had built, instead of running from feedback, I embraced it. I was secure enough to use it to my advantage to accomplish my goals. Women need to get comfortable not only asking for what they want, but asking what is it that they *didn't have* that prevented them from being sought out for an opportunity. We may go for that position we want and not get it. We may chalk it up to the Inner Critic, or I wasn't good enough anyway since I only had 60 percent of skills or experience required. Instead, go the extra mile and ask the hiring leader, 'I need feedback because the next time this opportunity presents itself, I would like to be a contender. What gaps did you see? What didn't I show you during the interview process that prohibited me from being a contender?' We have to ask those questions to grow. Sometimes you might think it's inappropriate, but we're going to stay where we are if we are afraid to seek out that feedback. When we are not selected, we need to know why and what we can do about it.

"I would give this advice to any woman: We have our networks. Make sure they are productive networks and not energy-zapping networks. Make sure to have a diverse portfolio of mentors because we need different mentors at different times in our lives. Seek coaching out if it is not given to you. We all need coaching in a lot of different instances—transitioning to a new role, professional development. If we have coaches really looking out for us and sponsors who will advocate for our success, they will be willing to give us the feedback we need. We have to be willing to receive it and do something with it. Lastly, sometimes we are our own worst enemy. Because we've not been given support, we're not bringing other women up and along with us. Even if we did have more women in leadership roles, we may still have a leaky pipeline or a gap. We have to change how we go about developing and empowering and building our community. Don't be self-serving, but be in service of others."

Still apprehensive about networking? Let's get practical. There are two activities you can do to condition for running over this hurdle.

CONDUCT A RELATIONSHIP AUDIT

The relationship audit is a tool that will help you take stock of who is in your orbit. The size of your current network may surprise you! Here's how to do it: Take out a piece of paper (or, if you're a fan, start an Excel spreadsheet). Make the following categories:

- **Family:** Defined as you wish, but inclusive of parents, siblings, cousins, aunts, uncles, spouse/partner, in-laws, spouse/partner family

- **Friends:** Relationships you have outside of your current workplace throughout your lifetime, such as friends from childhood and the community/communities in which you grew up, friends from high school, college, graduate school, community endeavors, former colleagues who you have stayed in touch with, etc.

- **Professional Contacts:** Those with whom you currently work, both inside your organization, such as peers, direct reports, your manager, others in the organization, and those professional relationships outside your organization, including, but not limited to, vendors, clients, and partners.

- **Community/Place of Worship/Other:** Those who may not fit in any of the categories above, but with whom you may socialize or see as you traverse through your life on the soccer field, at church, in yoga class, the grocery store, etc.

Now, start populating these categories with the people that come to mind. Welcome to your current vast network! Isn't it amazing how many people you already know? Creating a map of who you know is a great way to begin to think about the webs of networks in your life today. All of these people know other people. All of these people likely don't know you could use their help or support or connections to manifest what you want in your life. Once you have completed your map to your liking (I suggest you come back to it a few times and treat the map as a "living document" since, over time, you will think of others to add), you can continue with your relationship audit.

Using the list and categories of contacts you have created, it's time to determine how best to leverage them. This will require more thinking about the interests and capabilities of those on your map and how they align with your own.

When working with a leader recently on her relationship audit, the first thing we did was assign a number between 1–10 that depicted how close and comfortable she was with each person on her categorized contact list (1 = not very comfortable/close, 10 = very comfortable/close/easy to reach out to and make an ask of). We then sorted her map from 10–1, so those she had most ease and comfort level of relationship with ranked highest. This is where it helps to use Excel or another spreadsheet that you can easily sort. Next, we clearly articulated her goal: To move from her field of expertise (marketing) to one she hadn't worked in but wanted to move to (diversity and inclusion). Your goal can obviously be whatever you want. After depicting how much those on the list could help her accomplish her goal, it became clear for her, and will become clear for you when you take time to do this, who among her awesome and vast network of known relationships she should focus her time on as she began to manifest her vision.

As with all of the suggested activities in this book, you can modify the suggestions to make them work for you. You'll be on your way to thinking about your network in more strategic ways.

CREATE A NETWORKING PLAN

In addition to the list of all of those you identified in your current network, you will want to identify those with whom you don't have a relationship who you would like to know. Make your "want to get to know" wish list. Go ahead. Think big. Might your CEO or other members of your organization's executive team be able to help you? (Cue Inner Critic: "Seriously? She isn't going to take time with me! You're nuts!") Could the mother of one of your daughter's friends, who has the dream job you have always wanted, be someone you could tap despite never actually meeting her in person?

As you think about your networking plan, there are three factors you'll want to consider: a) being proactive, b) being open, and c) being smart about your time.

1. **Being proactive:** For being proactive with those you have identified as smart to connect with, how and when do you want to connect with some of these people (phone, coffee, lunch, skype, etc.)?

2. **Being open:** Means accepting outreach from others, or connecting with people even when there isn't a clear agenda; trusting that generative connection can result in fabulous outcomes. Generativity is simply being open to letting things transpire, or said a different way, leaving room for people and ideas to emerge in conversation.

3. **Being smart:** Being smart about your time will be the most important step and require you to get specific about how proactive and open you care to be at this moment in time. Having a clear intention, even if that intention is to be generative in the connection because you don't yet know the "why" behind the person you're connecting with, is a must.

As with asking, you may wish to think about your networking as micro commitments of time (a power half-hour via phone with a person who works in the field you wish to learn more about) and macro commitments of time (joining a nonprofit board or chairing a volunteer cross-functional committee at work that involves preparation and in-person meeting time).

I have a dare for you. Pick the highest-ranking person in your organization who you 1) wish to get on the radar of and 2) want to learn from. Think *big*. Think powerful. If the thought of reaching out to this person to ask for a coffee or a call doesn't make you a tad nervous, you're not thinking big enough. Be clear about your ask (30 minutes of time) and plan for the meeting when they say yes to you. Go willing to share your hopes, willing to share a bit about your superpowers, and with questions for them in hand. Let the discussion evolve. You have no idea what might transpire as a result.

TIME FOR SOCIAL NETWORKING?

Regarding your schedule, the clock—your professional one and the one tied to these hurdles—indicates that it is time to think of networking as a necessity, not an elective. Know that social media is an effective and efficient tool for building and leveraging relationships, not just producing and sharing content. A 2014 study by Ruby Media found that more women than men use Facebook (FB), Tumblr, Instagram, and Twitter.

Also, women overwhelmingly dominate Pinterest, a leisure platform that allows users to visually share and discover new interests. By contrast, more men than women use LinkedIn, the designated online professional networking site. This begs the question, why aren't more women maximizing the tools available to extend their professional reach.

Not planning my own time left me in a bit of a lurch recently with the people that matter most to me. Turns out, social media touch can only go so far in the "I care about you" department. Personal outreach still reigns supreme. Due in part to the fact that I am in the line of work I am in (not only does Linkage host large Institutes, but I am invited to speak frequently and may meet 400–1,000 leaders in an hour). With each person I meet, I get so curious and jazzed to know who they are and what they are up to. My genuine intention is to be available should they wish to connect further. But being in a people-focused business isn't an excuse for my lack of time management. Neither is having a big and open heart. In essence, frequency of touch matters, especially to those you deem most near and dear.

Increasingly, I have become more focused about with whom I spend my energy and time, ultimately balancing strategic relationship building to foster and manifest some of my own goals with tending to my closest family, friends, and colleagues. My desire to stay in frequent contact with the growing number of people I meet in my life is in stark contrast to the number of hours I have in my day. I am, if you haven't gleaned by now, a work in progress. What this has meant for me of late is being clear (daily) about my priorities, and saying yes and no to requests of my time with intention. I still hate to disappoint others. (I have confessed that I am a card-carrying member of the Over-Rowing Party, largely fueled by people pleasing.) Thankfully, practicing the tools suggested in this book has helped. For those who I care about (and need to show up for), I have made it a still-imperfect practice to reach out as often as I can. Some weeks, this narrows to phoning my mom, checking in with my brother, and of course ensuring time is reserved for my husband and kids. My apologies to friends (and even some colleagues) seem more frequent.

Your transparency about what you can and can't do will increasingly be met with forgiveness by those who you disappoint. Be aware of your time as you set out to foster your network. Your aim as you lift your head up from your to-do list and commit to building and leveraging your strategic network is to get better at it, not be perfect at it.

BRINGING IT ALL TOGETHER: YOUR RECIPE FOR SUCCESS

This chapter, like the last eight, has been designed for you to use on an ongoing basis and as your journey of self-discovery evolves. In so many ways, this final hurdle is the culminating hurdle. I believe that life happens in conversation. So, when you build and leverage relationships in your life, you will see the other hurdles emerge—and you will have the opportunity to scale them with intention. The secret to your success is recognizing which hurdles may be tripping you up and *Mastering Your Inner Critic*, and on some days, doing this on a moment-to-moment basis as you navigate your relationships. Here is your checklist, a helpful at-a-glance you can use before you connect with someone; a tool that will aid you in your leadership impact:

- Have I coached myself out of any harsh thinking to a place of compassion? Am I engaging in the world (in this conversation) from a place of compassion for myself and for others? Do I recognize that I am no better than and no less than the person with whom I am connecting? Am I being gentle as I glide?

- Am I clear about any deeply held beliefs that may no longer serve me? Am I confronting biases with curiosity and courage?

- Do I know what it is that I want in this moment, and if not, am I staying open to the possibility of what emerges?

- Have I stopped doing too much, putting down the oars long enough to do some work on ME? I'm worth it.

- Am I embracing my own strengths and wisdom, and bringing these unique attributes to my connections?

- What makes me fabulous? Am I playing to instill confidence in the areas I wish to be known for?

- Am I asking for what I really want—even when it's just for me and even if it's uncomfortable?

Gaining the clarity you need to get more of what you want in life means identifying, managing, and ultimately, mastering the hurdles that are holding you back. Use this book as your motivation, and when the going gets rough, reread the inspirational stories and practical wisdom from the awesome woman leaders featured in each chapter who have consciously developed the competence and needed shifts in mindset to overcome specific hurdles.

You've come this far. The world needs you and your leadership. And don't forget: We are all a masterpiece and a work in progress, simultaneously.

REFERENCES

INTERVIEWS

Barbara Annis. Phone interview. May 14, 2018.
Shannon Arnold. Phone interview. December 5, 2017.
Sarah Bettman. Phone interview. November 28, 2017.
Amy Shatto Bladen. Phone interview. December 15, 2017.
Joanne Brem. Phone interview. December 18, 2017.
Kim Cerda. Phone interview. May 24, 2018.
Yolanda Conyers. E-mail interview. December 1, 2017.
Yasmin Davidds. Phone interview. December 12, 2017.
Sabreen Dhillon. E-mail exchange. May 16, 2018.
Abri Holden. Phone interview. December 5, 2017.
Sonya Jacobs. Phone interview. December 13, 2017.
Sean Kavanaugh. Phone interview. March 12, 2018.
Richard Leider. Phone interview. April 3, 2018.
Melissa Master-Holder. Phone interview. December 1, 2017.
Kristy Roberts. Phone interview. December 1, 2017.
Stephanie Roemer. Phone interview. December 8, 2017.
Darlene Slaughter. Phone interview. March 22, 2018.
Cynthia Tragge-Lakra. Phone interview. December 17, 2017.
Tara Swart. Phone interview. April 5, 2018.
Margie Warrell. Phone interview. April 17, 2018.
Michelle Webb. Phone interview. December 8, 2017.
Madelyn Yucht. In person consultation and content review, on-going 2015–2018.

PUBLICATIONS

Adams, Merilee, and Marshall Goldsmith. *Change Your Questions, Change Your Life*. San Francisco: Berrett-Koehler Publishers, 2016.
Allen, Rita Balian. *Personal Branding and Marketing Yourself*. Waltham, MA: Balian Publishing Co. 2014.
Babcock, Linda, and Sarah Laschever. *Women Don't Ask*. Princeton, NJ: Princeton University Press, 2002.

Bateson, Gregory. *Steps to an Ecology of Mind.* Chicago: University of Chicago Press, 1972.

Bennis, Warren. *On Becoming a Leader.* New York: Basic Books, 2009.

Bergland, Christopher. "The Sweet Spot Between Hubris and Humility." Psychology Today. March 3, 2013. https://www.psychologytoday.com/us/blog/the-athletes-way/201303/the-sweet-spot-between-hubris-and-humility

Bohnet, Iris. *What Works.* Cambridge, MA: Belknap Press/Harvard University Press, 2016.

Brown, Brené. *The Gifts of Imperfection.* Center City, MN: Hazelden Publishing, 2010.

_____. *Rising Strong.* New York: Random House, 2017.

Center for Positive Organizations. Reflected Best Self Exercise™. http://positiveorgs.bus.umich.edu/cpo-tools/rbse/

Conyers, Yolanda, and Gina Qiao. *The Lenovo Way.* New York: McGraw-Hill Education, 2014.

Daley, Suzanne. "Little Girls Lose Their Self-Esteem Way to Adolescence, Study Finds." *New York Times.* January 9, 1991. (Archives) https://www.nytimes.com/1991/01/09/education/little-girls-lose-their-self-esteem-way-to-adolescence-study-finds.html

Davidds, Yasmin. *Your Own Terms.* New York: AMACOM, 2015.

Fang, Lily, and Sterling Huang. "Gender and Connections Among Wall Street Analysts." INSEAD. https://faculty.insead.edu/lily-fang/documents/working-paper_gender-and-connections.pdf

George, Bill. *Discover Your True North.* San Francisco: Jossey-Bass. 2015.

Goldsmith, Marshall. *What Got You Here Won't Get You There.* London: Profile Books, 2013.

Goleman, Daniel. *Emotional Intelligence.* New York: Bantam Books, 1995.

Hansen, Morten. *Great at Work.* New York: Simon & Schuster, 2018.

Harris, Carla. "Carla Harris Gives Career Advice to Her 25-Year-Old Self." Morgan Stanley. https://www.youtube.com/watch?v=y3YYCTf8YTU

Helgesen, Sally, and Marshall Goldsmith. *How Women Rise.* New York: Hachette Books, 2018.

Jarski, Verónica. "How Women and Men Use Social Media and Mobile." MarketingProfs. June 10, 2014. http://www.marketingprofs.com/chirp/2014/25327/how-women-and-men-use-social-media-and-mobile-infographic

Kahneman, Daniel. *Thinking, Fast and Slow.* New York: Farrar, Straus and Giroux, 2013.

Kaman, Vicki S., and Charmine E. J. Hartel. "Gender Differences in Anticipated Pay Negotiation Strategies and Outcomes." *Journal of Business and Psychology.* Vol. 9, No. 2 (Dec., 1994), pp. 183-197.

Kavanagh, Sean. "Leadership Presence." Ariel. March 22, 2018. https://info
.arielgroup.com/blog/the-definition-of-leadership-presence-an
-interview-with-ariel-ceo-sean-kavanagh

Kay, Katty, and Claire Shipman. *The Confidence Code*. New York: HarperBusiness, 2014.

_____. "The Confidence Gap." *The Atlantic*. May 2014.

Leider, Richard. *The Power of Purpose*. San Francisco: Berrett-Koehler Publishers, 2015.

_____. *Calling Cards*. Inventure—The Purpose Co. http://richardleider.com
/calling-cards/

_____, and David Shapiro. *Repacking Your Bags*. San Francisco: Berrett-Koehler Publishers, 2012.

Llopis, Glenn. "4 Skills that Give Women a Sustainable Advantage Over Men." *Forbes*. August 22, 2011.

Lubar, Kathy, and Belle Linda Halpern. *Leadership Presence*. New York: Avery, 2004.

Mayers, Juliette C. *A Black Woman's Guide to Networking*. Charleston, SC: CreateSpace, 2011.

_____. *The Guide to Strategic Networking*. Charleston, SC: CreateSpace, 2015.

Meyer, Eileen Hoenigman. "State of the Wage Gap." Glassdoor. April 4, 2017. https://www.glassdoor.com/blog/state-of-the-wage-gap-2017/

Patton, Bruce, Roger Fisher, and William Ury. *Difficult Conversations*. New York: Penguin Books, 2010.

_____, Douglas Stone, and Sheila Heen. *Getting to Yes*. New York: Penguin Books, 2011.

Peters, Tom. "The Brand Called You." *Fast Company*. August 31, 1997. https:
//www.fastcompany.com/28905/brand-called-you

Petri, Alexandra. "Famous Quotes the Way a Woman Would Have to Say Them During a Meeting." *The Washington Post*. October 13, 2015.

Semega, Jessica L., Kayla R. Fontenot, and Melissa A. Kollar. "Income and Poverty in the United States." Report No. P60-259. September 12, 2017. https://www.census.gov/library/publications/2017/demo/p60-259.html

Stanier, Michael Bungay. *The Coaching Habit*. Toronto: Box of Crayons, 2016.

Symons, Lesley, and Herminia Ibarra. "What the Scarcity of Women in Business Case Studies Really Looks Like." *Harvard Business Review*. April 2014.

Treanor, Jill. "Women Will Wait 217 Years for Pay Gap to Close, WEF Says." *The Guardian*. November 1, 2017. https://www.theguardian.com/society
/2017/nov/01/gender-pay-gap-217-years-to-close-world-economic
-forum

Warrell, Margie. *Find Your Courage*. New York: McGraw-Hill Education, 2009.

_____. *Stop Playing Safe*. Hoboken, NJ: Wrightbooks, 2013.

Wiseman, Liz, and Greg McKeown. *Multipliers.* New York: HarperBusiness, 2014.

Wood, Joanne V., W.Q. Elaine Perunovic, and John W. Lee. "Positive Self-Statements." *Psychological Science.* Volume 20—Number 7, pg. 860. 2009.

World Economic Forum. "2017 Global Gender Gap Report." November 2, 2017. https://www.weforum.org/reports/the-global-gender-gap-report-2017

WEBSITES

Barbara Annis—Gender Intelligence Group
http://www.genderintelligence.com/barbara-annis-associates/barbara-annis/

The Confidence Code
www.theconfidencecode.com

Equal Pay Negotiations, LLC
https://equalpaynegotiations.com

Good Judgment Project
https://www.iarpa.gov/index.php/newsroom/iarpa-in-the-news/2015/439-the-good-judgment-project

Harvard Negotiation Project
https://www.pon.harvard.edu/research_projects/harvard-negotiation-project/hnp/

Linkage Leadership and 360° Assessments
http://www.linkageinc.com/info/leadership-and-360-degree-assessments.cfm

Linkage Women in Leadership Institute™
http://www.linkageinc.com/institutes/women-in-leadership.cfm

Organizational Agility Advisors
https://orgagilityadvisors.com

Project Implicit
https://implicit.harvard.edu

Relational Life Institute
https://www.terryreal.com

Rosenberg's Self-Esteem Scale
https://www.wwnorton.com/college/psych/psychsci/media/rosenberg.htm

WhiteSpace at Work
http://www.whitespaceatwork.com

INDEX

ABOUT THE AUTHOR

 **Susan Mackenty Brady** inspires, educates, and ignites leaders globally on fostering a mindset of inclusion and self-awareness. As an expert in the advancement of women leaders, Susan advises C-level executives on how to create gender parity in organizations and motivates women to fully realize—and manifest—their leadership potential.

As EVP, Linkage Solutions, Susan oversees the growth of Linkage's two global solution areas: Purposeful Leadership & Advancing Women Leaders. She founded and now serves as co-chair of Linkage's Women in Leadership Institute, now in its 19th year and which boasts a network of over 10,000 alumni worldwide. Susan led the launch of Linkage's work in Advancing Women Leaders and Inclusive Leadership, and led the field research behind the 7 Leadership Hurdles Women Leaders Face in the Workforce™.

Susan is passionate about awakening the spirit of leaders the world over. She resides in the Boston area with her husband, two teenage daughters, and two Portuguese water dogs.